Letts**Guide**

Successful
Squash

Approved by the Women's Squash Rackets Association

Jane Poynder

National Coach, Women's Squash Rackets Association

WORLD OF SPORT

World of Sport is produced by
LWT for the ITV network.
This series is published in collaboration
with World of Sport by
Charles Letts & Co Ltd
London Edinburgh München & New York

First published 1980
Reprinted 1981
by Charles Letts & Co Ltd
Diary House, Borough Road, London SE1 1DW

Technical Editor: John Crooke
House Editor: Susan Meredith
Design: Perera
Illustrations: Sports Art Ltd
Colour photographs: All-Sport Photographic Ltd
Black and white photographs: Tim Pike (pp. 6, 12, 18, 25,
35-37, 41, 52-53, 70, 72, 74, 76) and Frank Newbould
(pp. 14, 22, 27-28, 30, 33, 41, 49-50), Dunlop Sports Co Ltd
(pp. 89, 90)
Cover shows Geoff Hunt (Australia) and Qamar Zaman (Pakistan)

ISBN 0 85097 442 9

Printed and bound by Charles Letts (Scotland) Ltd

Successful Squash

Sue Cogswell (Great Britain) in action on the forehand

Contents

The author

Introduction

So you want to play squash? Or perhaps you already play but need to improve your game. If you have not yet been in a squash court, have you ever thought what the game entails? All those white walls – that cell where people tear around in circles to emerge some short while later, hot and steamy, well exercised and full of *joie de vivre* – that is if they have won, of course. Your opponent beside you – not as a foe with the safety of a net between you, but right beside you – flailing a racket, taking up your space. What should you do? Is he really entitled to play a shot and then stand and prevent you from getting to the ball? Is it really so energetic – the floor space seems quite small – and what are those red lines on the floor and on the walls? Then, of course, there's the racket – not a very stout-looking weapon with such a long thin shaft and small head. Is it really possible to get it to meet that funny little lump of black dough called a ball?

Perhaps, however, you are all too familiar with these problems. You may have been playing squash for some time and now find that you have reached a plateau in your game and are unable to make any further improvement. Squash is a relatively easy game to take up but, like all sports, it requires a high level of skill, combined with rigorous practice and good coaching, if you are to reach the higher echelons.

This book has been written in the hope that it will help both the newcomer to the game and the more experienced player. It will not necessarily turn you into a Jonah Barrington or a Heather McKay – only a privileged minority can ever hope to scale those heights – but it will be a very practical guide to improving your performance, both technically and tactically, so that whatever your level of play you will enjoy the game more. In fact, this is what the game should be about – *fun, exercise* and, with luck, some *success*. Losing may be good for the soul, but winning is far better for your confidence.

Many newcomers to squash have had experience of other racket sports. This is good, although it may be necessary to adapt the techniques learnt in other games to those required on the squash court. People often ask if playing squash will damage their tennis, their badminton or their golf. You seldom hear a musician asking if playing the piano will damage his skill at the violin. Providing you realise that there are some fundamental differences and that adaptation will be necessary, knowledge of other sports can only be an advantage, particularly where patterns of movement, tactics, competitive attitudes, etc. are concerned.

Another attraction squash has for beginners is that they are able to get enjoyment and exercise, and achieve some measure of success, right from the outset. Provided you are well matched with your opponent in standard, you should be able to play some form of game on your first visit to the squash court. There is no restricting net to clear and the ball has only to hit the front wall somewhere between the boundary line and the tin – quite a vast expanse!

However, don't be led astray by this comparatively easy beginning, and don't assume you should always play a game when in the court. That old adage 'practice makes perfect' certainly applies to squash, and that is why this book will show you not only what you should be trying to do on the court, but also *how to practise,* whether on your own, with a partner, or in a group lesson. Either individual or group coaching will help too, but do remember that no coach has a magic wand to turn you into a good player overnight. One lesson a week with another ten hours' practice would be the ideal. In short, there is no easy road to instant success, but with a well balanced approach to practice, coaching and competitive play, *everyone* should be able to improve their standard. Above all, enjoy your squash. It is a fascinating game and should give you many hours of frustration and pleasure! Join the addicts.

Chapter 1 The game of squash

Points to consider before you begin

Booking a court

Squash, as everyone knows, is a booming game – if you have actually managed to book a squash court you score your first point. Court time is at a premium, clubs and sports centres are invariably full to overflowing during the popular hours between 5.00 p.m. and 10.00 p.m., so you must not expect to stay on a court for as long as you would like. Most court bookings last between thirty and sixty minutes; the average is forty-five minutes, which is an ideal time for a good game. You must vacate your court the moment you hear that bang on the door to say your time is up. Time really does mean money, particularly in the peak periods.

However, many clubs are comparatively empty during the day and sometimes offer cheaper rates, particularly in school holidays, so if you hear that your local club is full, do enquire whether they run some form of restricted membership for daytime players. Many also cater for squash playing mothers with young children, who can often be safely occupied in a club run *crèche* for an hour or so. Business men often find a lunch hour playing squash better for the waistline than the expense account meal, and better for overall fitness as well.

Equipment

There are certain disadvantages to playing a game in a cell. All too often, beginners find that their weapon has a nasty habit of coming into wounding contact with the walls. So, when selecting a racket, choose one that is not too heavy, feels good in your hand and, if it is to become a trusted friend, beware of those walls. There are obviously a number of other technical points to consider when purchasing a racket, such as type of shaft, handle and stringing, but fuller details concerning equipment will be considered later (Chapter 8).

Clothing should be comfortable and preferably absorbent. The rules of the game state that players must be attired predominantly in white, although some sports centres do waive this rule. Shoes are of extreme importance. They are your tyres, so check them well, and avoid bringing the wrath of court owners and managers upon your head by ensuring that you have non-marking soles. Black rubber soles are forbidden.

The ball

The ball very often presents problems, because the pace selected is wrong for the court conditions or the standard of the players. There are four paces of squash ball. Study the table below and select a ball suitable for both the court conditions and your standard of play.

	Yellow dot *Super slow*	White dot *Slow*	Red dot *Medium*	Blue dot *Fast*
Top tournament players	Tournament play	Very cold courts	For simulating hot court conditions on very cold courts	
County players	County play	Cold courts	For simulating hot court conditions on very cold courts	
Average club players	Hot courts	Cold courts	Very cold courts	
Beginners	Not recommended	Warm courts	Cold or very cold courts	

A squash ball should be quite bouncy once you have hit it for two or three minutes, and the harder you hit it, the warmer and bouncier it will become. The balls come in three colours – black, and the two non-marking shades of green and blue. Many clubs and sports centres allow the use of only the non-marking balls in their courts, so check on this before purchasing and preferably buy two. They do have a habit of splitting, so it is always advisable to carry a spare.

Fig. 1 The court

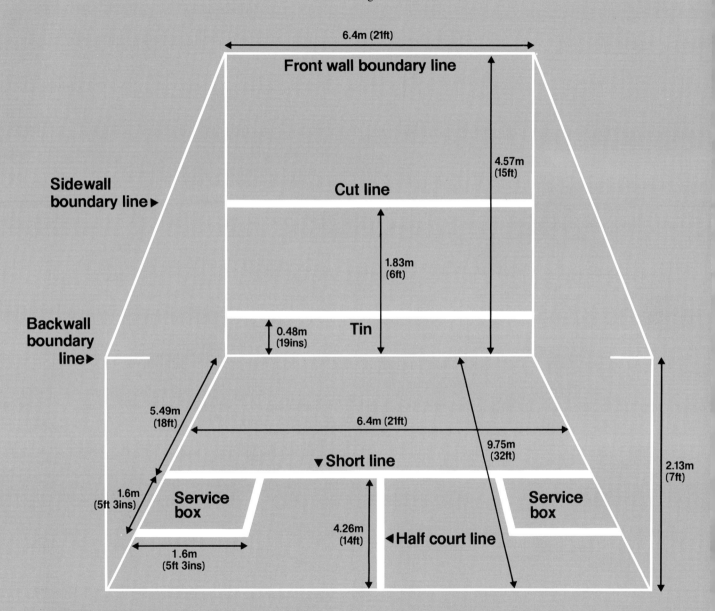

The court

You will discover that squash courts vary tremendously in play and feel, although the basic dimensions are the same. The court is a white, walled rectangle with a front wall, two sidewalls and a back wall, which may sometimes be made of glass. The dimensions of the court, the line markings on the walls and floor are indicated in Fig. 1.

The height of the squash court may vary, as may the light fittings and even the type of lights used. Many older courts have globe bulbs, whereas new courts usually have six double, fluorescent tubes. Older courts also tend to have fixed beams, so remember that if you hit between these beams you will lose the rally. The floor is made of hard wood, often maple, and again this can vary from court to court. Some floors may be very highly varnished, which can make them rather slippery. The temperature of courts varies considerably, and the warmer the court, the faster and more bouncy the ball becomes. The temperature is one of the first things you should notice about a court; whatever your standard, the speed of the court will have some effect on your game.

The aim of the game

Squash is usually played by two people, although there are rules for the doubles game and a number of special doubles courts (see Chapter 7).

The ball is struck alternately by the players before the bounce or after the bounce, and must touch the front wall between the boundary line and the tin, although, apart from in the service, it may go via any of the other walls. Only the server, known as 'hand in', scores a point when winning a rally. 'Hand out', the receiver, wins only the service when winning a rally.

The first player to score nine points wins the game and a match usually consists of the best of five games. Women play the same number of games as men, unlike in tennis. If the score reaches eight all, 'hand out', the receiver, may then decide whether the game is to be played to nine or ten points, either 'no set' or 'set two' respectively. The game never goes beyond ten points.

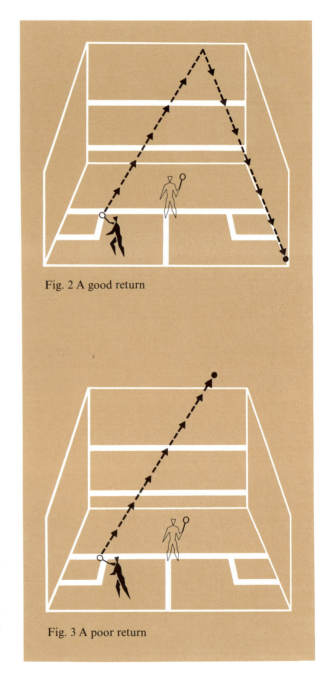

Fig. 2 A good return

Fig. 3 A poor return

10

Geoff Hunt (Australia) shaping up for a forehand

Safety

Squash is one of the few racket sports in which your opponent is beside you. So, having played a shot, you *must* get out of the way to let your opponent play his. If either of you feel you do not have room to swing your racket, then *stop* and play the point again. If you think you may hit your opponent with the ball, again stop and replay the point. Chapter 7 deals with the rules of the game, particularly those concerning obstructions, lets and penalty points, but in the early stages of your squash career, do get into the habit of stopping whenever there is an obstruction (Fig. 4). This will ensure your safety, add to your enjoyment and stand you in good stead when, and if, you become a serious match competitor.

Another point to consider regarding safety and your well-being is your age, when playing squash for the first time. People often take up squash when in the twenty to thirty age group, some even later. It is wise, therefore, to remember that squash is an extremely energetic game and if you have been unused to taking any very strenuous form of exercise, do follow these simple points:

a) If you are in the 'mature' age group, take reasonable precautions to ensure that you are fit enough to play squash, and try not to push yourself too hard too soon – you want to be around to enjoy your club membership.

b) Always do some sort of loosening up before you go on court, even if it is only a little jogging on the spot, arm circling, etc. It is particularly unwise to go on a cold court without limbering up; the result is often injury, torn muscles, twisted ankles, or worse. In cold conditions start off in a tracksuit. You can always shed it before the match begins.

c) If you wear glasses it is wise to have plastic lenses.

The first attempt in the squash court

You may be one of the lucky minority who has a natural ball sense, that ability to react with ease to a moving ball to produce a good shot. However, not all newcomers to squash have this natural aptitude so, if you find difficulty in getting ball and bat to meet, here are a few basic exercises which may be of some help.

You have to come to terms with the length of the racket, so take hold of it, put the ball on the strings

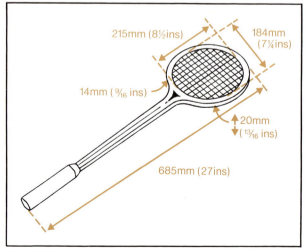

Fig. 4 Obstruction

Fig. 5 The racket

and then, keeping the ball and racket head a comfortable distance away from you, gently tap the ball up in the air. Once you are able to do this, move towards the front wall and gently tap the ball onto the wall. Gradually move back and when the ball seems a little warmer, allow it to bounce on the floor before you make your swing. See how high on the wall you can aim, concentrating all the time on keeping the racket head a comfortable distance away from you. Try not to allow the head of the racket to drop, but tilt the racket face 'open' slightly so that you hit under the ball. This will give it more height on the front wall.

Ideally you and your partner should have a ball each for these simple warm-up exercises. As your co-ordination improves, move further back towards the short line and see if you can hit the ball onto the front wall so that it lands in the imaginary channel made between the sidewalls and the line of the service box running parallel to the sidewall (Fig. 6). To get this straight direction of the shot try to turn sideways, so that you are facing the sidewall as you play your shot. Assuming you are right-handed, you should be play-

ing forehands down the right-hand side of the court, and backhands down the left. (All instructions in this book will be for the right-handed player. Left-handers should therefore adapt them to their viewpoint.) Always make certain you are keeping a good distance away from the sidewall. The channels of the court should be for the ball – not for you.

Once you have achieved some success at this individual rallying, see if you and your partner are able to keep a rally going with each other. One of you should stand just outside the service box on the right-hand side and the other in the equivalent position on the left. Aim your shot towards the centre of the front wall above the cut line, so that it comes back within easy reach. Again concentrate on keeping yourself out of the two side channels. The ball may go from the front wall towards the sidewall. If this happens, try not to rush towards the sidewall. Allow the ball to bounce off the wall and then play your stroke (Fig. 7). As your rally with each other improves, try to change the direction of your shot by first hitting above the cut line and then below the cut line. This will begin to move your

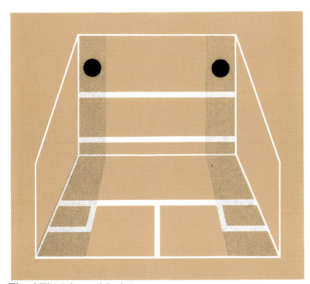

Fig. 6 The 'channels' of the court

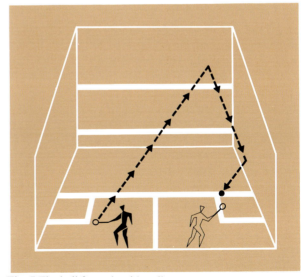

Fig. 7 The ball from the sidewall

13

opponent up and down the court. If you are on the left-hand side of the half court line, do remember to play a backhand. It may be tempting to run round the ball and play the shot on your stronger wing, but this will prove disastrous in the long term. Always remember to *keep away from the walls.*

Now you may like to progress to some form of a game. The service boxes on the floor are only for standing in when serving. Spin the racket to see who should serve. The winner of the toss chooses from which service box to begin. To serve, toss the ball in the air to the side of you and see if you can hit it before it bounces. Your service should hit high on the front wall, above the cut line but below the boundary line, so that it bounces in your opponent's back quarter of the court, avoiding both the short line and the half court line. (See Chapter 3 for a full explanation of the service.)

The 'T' position

Having served the ball to your opponent, move immediately to the 'T' position on the court, assuming that you have managed to get your service into the correct area (Fig. 8). If you play your shot into the middle of the court it will be impossible for you to move to this central position, so aim your service well. The 'T' is the best position on the court, the area from which you should be able to reach all shots with comparative ease (Fig. 9). Your opponent should try to remove you from this area by playing the return well away from the middle of the court. The rally should then proceed with both of you trying to play the ball away from each other, and away from the centre of the court. Remember that if your shots bounce in the middle you are putting your opponent in the most advantageous position—an unwise move.

In the early stages pay particular attention to where you aim your shot on the front wall, and always remember to keep well away from the side-walls. The channels of the court are for the ball, the rectangle in the middle of the court is for the bodies!

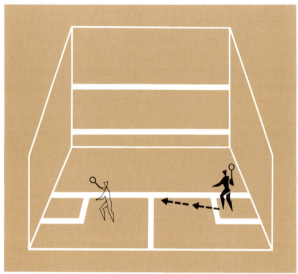

Fig. 8 Movement to the 'T' position

Fig. 9 Watching the ball from the 'T'

Good backhand preparation from Mohibullah Khan (Pakistan)

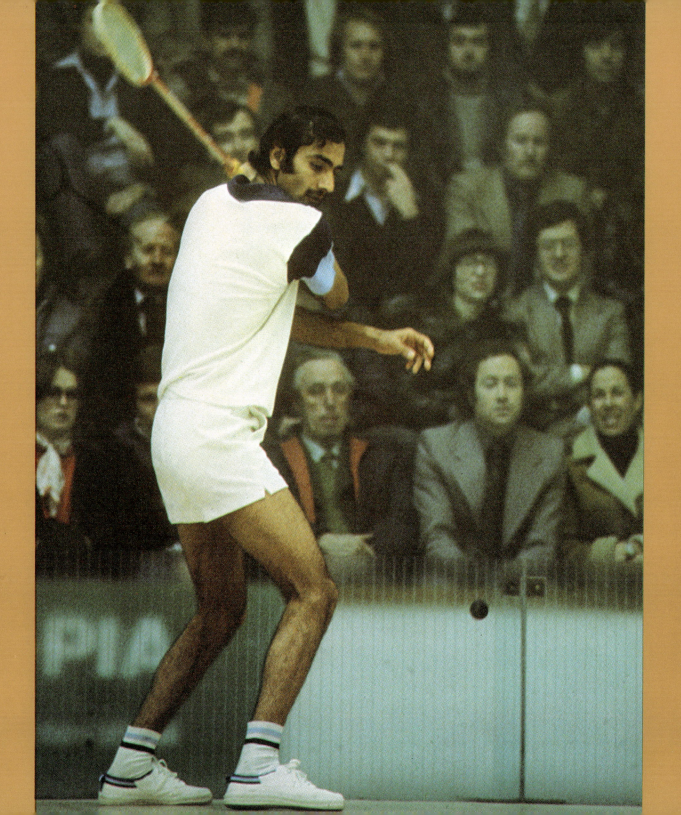

Chapter 2 The road to improvement

In the early stages of squash, too much technical instruction becomes confusing and can spoil the initial enjoyment of trying to get bat and ball to coincide. However, after the first trial session, it is essential for all novices to the game to start playing in as technically correct a manner as possible. There are a number of fundamental points common to all strokes in squash and these should form the basis for all technical improvements. Try to use the following as a check-list when developing any new skill.

Stroke fundamentals
1 The grip
2 The importance of watching the ball
3 The position of the body in relation to the ball
4 Control of the swing of the racket and the face of the racket
5 Good movement and balance throughout the shot
6 Recovery for the next shot.

Strokes often go wrong because one of the fundamentals is incorrect. So, the more attention you pay to these details at an early stage, the sounder your stroke production will become. All the fundamentals are inter-linked, so if you work through them logically you should help yourself to improve. Fault correction must be specific and simple.

The grip
One of the good points about squash is that there is only one grip to be used for all strokes, but it is therefore all the more necessary to get it right from the very beginning.

The squash grip is often referred to as a 'shake hands grip' or a 'continental grip'. Hold the shaft of the racket in your non-playing hand, with the racket at right angles to the ground. Place your racket hand over the handle so that the thumb and forefinger form a 'V' which points up the shaft of the racket (Fig. 10A). Spread your fingers round the back of the handle using a slightly wider spread of the index finger, as if it was spread round the trigger of a pistol (Fig. 10B). The thumb should be lying diagonally,

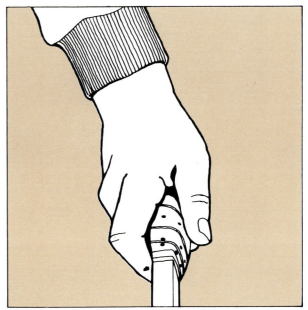
Fig. 10A

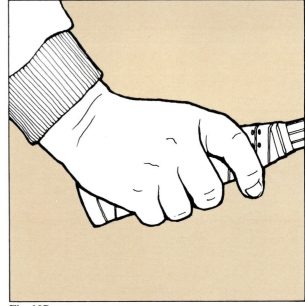
Fig. 10B

across the back of the handle (Fig. 10C). The hand should be approximately 5mm ($\frac{1}{4}$ in) from the butt of the handle; this may vary slightly as a matter of preference, but, remember, the shorter your grip the less reach you will have on your shots.

Feel as if you are moulding your hand to the handle. The inexperienced player tends to hold the racket far too tightly and this results in lack of control of the racket head. Your grip is your control column, enabling you to feel the ball on the racket, and giving you flexibility as well as control, much needed in basic stroke production. In the early stages you may find you tend to lose this new grip, reverting to forehand and backhand, but do persevere. The more proficient you become the faster the game becomes and the less time you will have to move your hand. Many players with a tennis background find this one of the most difficult lessons to learn.

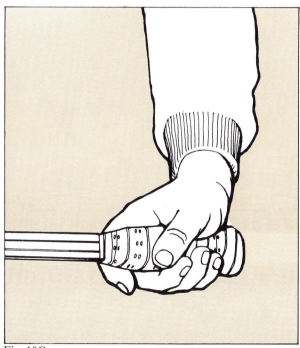

Fig. 10C

The importance of watching the ball

One of the simplest tactics in squash is to try to move to the centre of the court – the 'T' position – having put your opponent in a position at the back of the court. Both your opponent *and the ball* are then behind you, and it is essential that you know what the one is about to do with the other. Turn and watch the ball. You will then know where to move for your next stroke and, with a little experience, you will begin to know, from the way your opponent shapes up to play a shot, what type of stroke he is about to make. Your anticipation and movement towards the ball will thus improve. It is also essential to watch the ball as you, yourself, are playing the shot – an obvious point, but one that is often overlooked when the heat is on in a fast rally.

The position of the body in relation to the ball

If you are not used to wielding a racket, one of the most difficult lessons to learn is getting used to the distance between the racket head and racket handle. Often, novices rush the stroke, get far too close to the ball and also far too close to the side and back walls.

It is important to remember that, when striking the ball on either the basic forehand or backhand, the racket needs to be extended a comfortable distance away from the body, with the ball being struck at approximately knee height (Fig. 11). By striding into the shot, you increase your reach, so allow for this.

Control of the swing of the racket and the face of the racket

A good swing is an important asset to a squash player, as the swing is common to all strokes, unlike in many sports, which require differing technical actions.

There are, of course, slight variations on the basic squash swing, but the following fundamental points should always be attended to when trying to perfect the swing (Fig 12):

a) the backswing and preparation for the shot,
b) the pathway forwards towards the point of impact, with concentration on the cocked wrist and the high, but bent, elbow,

Fig. 11A Correct extension of the racket

Fig. 11B Incorrect extension of the racket

c)   the follow through.

Squash is often referred to as a 'wristy' game. Do not be confused by this and think it means that you need a loose, wristy flick when you hit the ball. Rather, think of squash as a forearm game, where the wrist is cocked in order to put more throwing power into the shot.

As well as the pathway of the racket, you must learn to control the face of the racket, namely the angle at which the racket meets the ball. Most shots in squash are hit with a slightly open racket face, which puts a little underspin or cut on the ball. To gain maximum height on a shot such as a lob, you turn the racket face even more, i.e. open to the maximum, to lift the ball high. The racket face is closed when the player hits over the top of the ball with a form of top spin. This is not a spin used very much in squash, although it does appear occasionally at the highest level.

Fig. 12 The swing

– backswing and preparation
– towards the point of impact
– follow through

Good movement and balance throughout the shot

An essential part of good technique is a player's movement to and from a shot. Although the floor area is comparatively small, the good squash player must cover the court in as economical a way as possible. Every unnecessary step takes its toll over the period of five games. You should really be no more than three strides away from any shot. So, try to develop a fairly long stride as you move towards the ball, making the longest stride as you step in to play the shot. Rock back on this stride in a form of 'rocker' motion as you begin your return movement towards the 'T'. Remember it helps to keep in a slightly crouched position, with the racket head up and your knees flexed, ready to sprint off in the required direction. Beware of standing too upright on the squash court; you will never move off sufficiently quickly to pick up those low shots in the front of the court.

At a high level of play you will often see players taking many shots off the so-called 'wrong foot'. Why then are you being encouraged always to turn and step in on the correct, leading foot? The answer is that, under extreme pressure, it is often more effective tactically to lunge out on the wrong foot, *providing your balance is correct*. The better player gets away with this short cut on his footwork, but the novice, not in full control of his balance, often allows his shot to fail when played in this way. Assuming you have time enough, always turn correctly, and when under extra pressure only allow yourself to step in on the wrong foot if your body turn and balance are still correct.

Recovery for the next shot

Players often spoil their stroke because they try to force the pace of the shot by twisting their body as they hit, or are so anxious to recover to the 'T' position that they fail to complete their stroke before moving. Try to avoid these pitfalls yourself. Concentrate on completing the stroke and then moving rapidly back to the 'T' with those economical strides. Recovery from one shot is preparation for the next, so prepare well.

Simple exercises to help develop control

Good squash is about good ball and racket control. It should not be a question of 'bash and dash'. To help you develop the necessary control, try some of the following exercises.

1 Stand in the area beside the right-hand service box and see if you can play the ball continuously down the channel between the sidewall and the service box line. Avoid hitting the ball too hard and low – see if, by opening the racket face, you are able to get the ball to hit the front wall above the cut line. As your control improves, count the number of strokes that bounce back in the service box area. Progress to the same practice on the backhand. (By using two balls both you and your partner can practise like this at the same time.) Always have a particular target area on the front wall. In your mind, liken the front wall to a draught board and concentrate on the particular square at which you are aiming.

One of the first objectives in squash is to hit the ball to a good *length* but, rather than thinking of the length itself, try to think of the way to achieve it. *Height* will give you *depth* in the court, and this height is achieved by opening the racket face and getting a good swing with the racket.

2 As your control improves, continue this rally up and down the sidewall, but now bring in your partner so that you hit the ball in turn. Begin with one of you, player A, standing behind the service box, setting the ball up in the front of the court for the other, player B, to play a length forehand to the back corner (Fig. 13). Then progress to a rally with both players trying to play the ball into the channel of the service box. This will mean that you now require more movement to and from the 'T'. (Remember to stop if you are likely to hit your opponent with either the racket or ball.)

In this exercise pay particular attention to the pattern of your movement between shots. It is up to every player who has just struck the ball to give the opponent the *direct* route to the ball. There-fore, when you have played the ball from behind the service box, you must move round the back of your opponent before coming forward to the 'T' (Fig.14).

3   Progress to a game, but try as much as possible to keep the ball out of the rectangle of the court formed by the service box lines (Fig. 15). This will enable you to move to and from the 'T' quite freely.

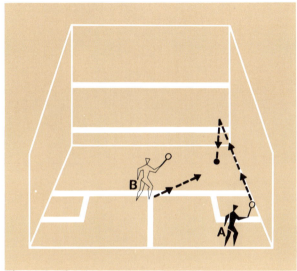

Fig. 13 Feeding for a length shot

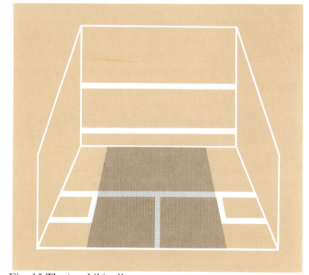

Fig. 15 The 'prohibited' area

Fig. 14 Movement to clear the ball

Even in your first game, bear in mind the following *tactics*, which form the basis of a good game at all levels:

a)   Play the ball away from the centre of the court and to the back of the court, near the back corners.

b)   Move to the 'T', having placed your opponent and the ball away from the 'T'.

c)   Think of the game as having four main target areas, the four corners of the court, and try to play your shot to one of these corners, preferably the one furthest away from your opponent.

Chapter 3 **Good stroke production**

Good technique is not an end in itself. However, the better your technique in a game, the more chance you have of being able to put your tactics to good effect. It is therefore worth spending some time developing a good grounding in all the basic strokes.

The forehand drive to a length

The aim of this shot is to hit the ball parallel to, and preferably hugging, the sidewall, so that it bounces at the back of the court and dies in the back corner. The length shot is the foundation on which your whole game depends – if played well, it prevents your opponent from gaining an attacking position and allows you to dictate the course of the rally.

To achieve a good forehand, concentrate on the following points:

a) *Preparation of the racket*

Note that the head of the racket is held high with the racket face slightly open. The elbow should be bent but lifted high so that as the racket comes forward the forearm is able to move the head of

Fig. 16B The forehand drive – impact

Fig. 16A The forehand drive – preparation

Fig. 16C The forehand drive – follow through

the racket through towards the point of impact with a type of throwing action (Fig. 16A).

b) *Impact area*

Try to strike the ball on a line with the leading foot, at approximately knee height. The ball for an attacking drive should be roughly at the top of its bounce, perhaps just over the top of the bounce if you want to delay your stroke. To get your body weight into the shot, step in on your leading foot as you strike the ball (Fig. 16B).

c) *Follow through*

For a full follow through feel as if you need to keep the ball on the racket as long as possible. The ball will go where your racket head and leading shoulder end up pointing. Therefore, to play a successful straight shot, you must remain sideways throughout the stroke. *Do not pull round* as you strike the ball. This will pull your shot down the centre of the court (Fig. 16C).

Practice for the forehand drive to a length

Individual

1   Count the shots in a rally on the right-hand side of the court.
2   Develop the rally so that you hit:
    a) above the cut line,
    b) above the cut line, but down the channel of the half court,
    c) above the cut line, but bouncing in the service box,
    d) bouncing beyond the service box.

Once you have achieved a reasonable amount of control at the easy practice, you should try to set yourself more difficult targets by reducing the target area. Remember the important fundamental of foot-work and in all these exercises make certain you are moving your feet correctly, stepping into each shot as you play it. There are two ways to practise – well or badly – and if you practise badly, you will only consolidate your faults and make them even more difficult to alter.

Pairs

1   Set up a shot in the front of the court so that the partner on the 'T' is able to move in and play a length shot down the right-hand sidewall. As your control improves, set up the ball closer to the front wall so that the partner on the 'T' really has to stride in to reach it. Think of the pattern of your movement when striding in for this short shot. Two small strides and then one long stride out on the left foot should be sufficient, with that rocker motion back to the right foot as you return to the 'T'. Also remember to watch the ball as it bounces in the back of the court. *There should be no time in squash when you are not in sight of the ball.* By turning to see where your ball has landed you will also be more likely to remain sideways throughout your shot – a prerequisite of any successful straight length shot.

2   Develop this length shot with both partners playing to the area of the service box, but now bring in the movement to and from the 'T'. Try to co-operate with each other in the early stages to improve your ball control. Concentrate on:
    a) a compact swing both on preparation and follow through (to avoid injury),
    b) the correct movement pattern to and from the 'T'.

3   Finally progress to a game, using only the right-hand half of the court. As your control improves, restrict the area you allow yourself. The ultimate aim would be the area behind the service box, about 15cm (6ins) from the sidewall, but work up to this gradually.

The forehand drive cross court

Your straight length shots may be your 'bread and butter' shots, but it is also important to be able to hit the ball successfully across the court. Technically, the swing for this shot is similar to that for the straight shot, but there are two main differences:

23

a) The ball should be struck slightly in front of the leading foot.

b) You should open your stance more so that the ball will naturally end up across the court. Again remember that the ball will go where your racket and leading shoulder end up pointing, and concentrate on that target area on the front wall.

A good cross court shot must have good *width*, as its aim is to remove your opponent from the 'T'. Very often newcomers to the game tend to play the majority of their shots across the court by mistake, often straight to the opponent, simply because they have failed to keep sideways when attempting a straight shot. Try not to fall into this trap.

Practice for the forehand drive cross court

Pairs

1 Both players hit to each other across the court, first aiming to get the ball to bounce in the opposite back quarter, then progressing to the service box, and finally to behind the service box.

2 Player A should stand on the 'T' with player B in the back left-hand corner. B should set the ball up in the right-hand front corner for A to move in to play the shot back across the court. Again, as the front player, you should concentrate on that economy of movement with the long stride in on the left foot as you play the shot, and the rocker motion back on the right foot. Allow the body to turn slightly as you play the ball across the court, and again watch to see your ball bounce in the back of the court.

The backhand drive to a length

At the beginning it is often more difficult to hit a good backhand than a good forehand. After all, if you are going to strike someone with the hand, you naturally slap with the palm rather than using the back of the hand, as the palm tends to be stronger. However, once you have mastered the technique of a backhand, it can often become a safer shot than the forehand with fewer problems. Again the aim of the basic backhand is that elusive length. To achieve this, concentrate on the following points (Fig. 17):

a) Racket preparation – high, cocked wrist, bent elbow, with shoulders practically facing the left-hand back corner.

b) Impact area – the ball should be struck on a line with the right knee, a comfortable distance to the side. The racket face should be slightly open to lift the ball onto the front wall. Again concentrate on stepping into the ball to get your weight behind the shot.

c) The follow through should finish high, again with bent elbow.

Problems

a) Try not to allow the wrist to drop. If it does, you will push the ball and consequently lose power.

b) Remember that your speed of shot comes from the successful swing of the racket and transfer of weight from left to right foot on the point of impact. Do not allow yourself to force this power by moving your body too much as you strike the ball. This will only pull the shot off course, and invariably the ball will then land in the middle of the court for your opponent to put away.

Practice for the backhand drive to a length

Individual

1 Count the shots in a rally on the backhand – first in the full left-hand half of the court, and then down the channel, aiming to get the ball to land in the service box. Aim well above the cut line to achieve a good length.

2 Vary the height at which you hit the ball onto the front wall and narrow down your target area in the channel. Count the number of shots you achieve in any one rally. This gives you an incentive and helps concentration.

Fig. 17 The backhand drive – preparation, impact, follow through

Pairs

1   Set up a backhand on the left-hand side of the court for the player in front to move from the 'T' and play a length shot. Repeat, bringing in continuous feeding as the backhand improves.

2   Progress to a rally as used on the forehand, with the service box as the target area and both players moving in a circle to and from the 'T'. In the early stages co-operate with each other to build up a successful rally.

3   Progress to a game, with both players now trying to score points, but still keeping the ball on the left-hand half of the court.

In all these exercises for the backhand, do make sure that you play a backhand. It is all too easy to be tempted to run round the shot and play a forehand, but this only means that you will end up pinned against the left-hand sidewall. The sooner you become confident on the backhand wing the better.

You should also notice the importance of the high follow through with a bent elbow. If you are still driving the ball through with a straight arm, you are a danger to your opponent, and players with dangerous swings may be disqualified when they reach the stage of competitive squash, so be warned. It is essential to develop an effective, but safe, swing.

Practice for combined forehand and backhand

When attempting these exercises, try to work through the following stages – *control, co-operation* and *competition*. Concentrated and serious practice needs precise targets and guidelines, both to keep your interest and to make the exercise worthwhile. Never forget the fundamentals of good *footwork* and good *positioning* for the stroke.

If you are lucky enough to find a court which you can use on your own, try the exercise below. Remember, if you are working alone you will have twice as many hits – twice the chance of improving your shots.

Individual

Hit one straight forehand down the sidewall towards the right-hand service box, play the next shot across the court to the left-hand service box, run across and play a straight shot down the left-hand wall, and then play the fourth shot as a cross court backhand. Repeat the exercise, scoring a point each time you succeed in completing the sequence of four shots. Lose a point when you fail on the sequence. Try not to lose to yourself by failing to do the required sequence exactly. You can add variety to the exercise by increasing the number of straight shots you play. Always try to keep to the number of shots you set yourself.

Pairs

As a warm-up, use the exercises already given for both forehand and backhand and then progress to one of the following:

1   Play a set number of length forehands, then a cross court shot, followed by a set number of length backhands. Repeat.

Note: If you use an odd number of straight shots, the same person will play the cross court shot on each side. If you use an even number of straight shots, play will alternate on the cross court shot. For example: Player A plays a forehand length; player B plays a forehand length; player A plays a cross court; player B plays a backhand length; player A plays a backhand length and player B plays a cross court.

2   Use the same exercise but allow one player to choose when to play the cross court shot. This will emphasise the need to watch the ball the whole time. Remember the basic tactic of keeping the ball out of the middle of the court, and in all these exercises try to keep it in the two side channels.

Conditioned practice games

A conditioned practice game is one in which either one or both of the players are 'conditioned', i.e. restricted to playing a particular type of shot to a particular area of the court. It is often the competitive extension of a set practice.

As a warm-up, play the games already suggested for forehand and backhand practice, using only one half of the court and reducing your area as control improves. Then progress to the following:

1   Play a conditioned game using both cross court and straight shots, but allowing the ball to bounce only in the two side channels.

2   Play a conditioned game, as above, but keep the ball behind the short line and in the two side channels.

3   To help one player develop a good basic game, restrict him to playing every shot down the nearest sidewall, while allowing the opponent to play any shot he likes. This will instil the need, when under pressure, to play to a safe length.

4   For a player who needs to persevere with length, make the condition such that he has to play every shot behind the short line, whereas the opponent may play whatever stroke he likes.

Change roles at the end of each game.

The service

The service is the means of starting a rally. The server, known as 'hand in', must stand with at least one foot completely within the service box. The ball must be struck before it touches the floor, must be hit directly onto the front wall between the boundary line and the cut line and must land in the opposite back quarter of the court, avoiding both the short line and the half court line. For the exact rules on service see Chapter 7.

The aim of the service should be to put the opponent under considerable pressure, preventing him from playing a winning return and keeping him on the defensive.

There are many different types of serve, but perhaps the most useful are the high lob and the hard length. Develop these first, but consider the variations later. It is never wise to be too predictable.

Before serving concentrate on the following points:

a)   Take up a good position in the service box, with one foot entirely within the box, but as near to the 'T' as possible.

b)   Any service is a cross court shot, so open your stance so that your left shoulder is pointing towards your target area on the front wall (Fig. 18).

c)   Take your time. Look at your opponent and check that he is ready. This is the one occasion in squash

Fig. 18A Serving from the right-hand box

Fig. 18B Serving from the left-hand box

Fig. 19 Angle of service from the right-hand box

Fig. 20 Angle of service from the left-hand box

when he is unable to rush you, but neither must you rush him by serving too quickly; he would then be quite within his rights to refrain from hitting the ball, and a let would have to be played.

d) You should have only two quick strides to make to reach the 'T', so move as soon as you have hit the ball, and you are then established in the attacking position.

e) Finally, remember to watch the ball as it travels to the back corner. It is essential that you know what your opponent is about to do with the return.

The lob service

The lob service is very similar to the basic forehand drive, but with great emphasis on an open racket face to achieve the required height on the front wall.

Toss the ball well to the side of you, and then swing your racket through, lifting the ball onto the front wall as near the top boundary line as possible. When serving from the right-hand service box, aim some 30cm (12ins) to the left of the centre of the wall (Fig. 19). From the left-hand box, widen the corresponding angle slightly (Fig. 20). Your exact target area will depend on the temperature and speed of the court, but use these suggestions as a guideline.

Concentrate on a good transfer of weight from right to left foot as you serve, and then take those two quick strides to the 'T'.

The hard length service

The ball on this harder service should travel towards the required area fairly fast, and should end up touching the sidewall low down near the back of the service box, before travelling on towards the back of the court. This forces the receiver to play the ball after it has bounced and the shot is often difficult to return because of its speed. A variation in direction may be used as a surprise measure, either by aiming straight at the opponent or by playing the ball so that it travels down the middle of the court near the half court line.

When playing the hard length serve, take up a similar position in the service box as for the lob serve but, instead of aiming the ball high on the front wall, use a higher swinging action, striking the ball at approximately shoulder level, and aim to hit the wall just above the cut line (Fig. 21). Again move to the 'T' after serving, but beware of moving too soon if you decide to play the serve down the middle, as you might then be obstructing your opponent.

Practice for the lob and hard length service

For either of these serves set yourself a target area and count the number of successful hits. Practise from both boxes and move to the 'T' after serving.

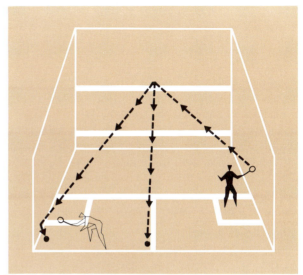

Fig. 21 The hard length service

Progress to working with a partner, the server scoring every time the receiver fails to return a correct service. Have ten serves and then change roles. Remember, the most important requirements on service are consistency and accuracy.

The backhand service

The main advantage of a backhand service is that you can use it from the right-hand service box without having to turn your back on your opponent.

The backhand serve is similar to the basic backhand. The server starts with the left foot in the service box and transfers his weight to the right foot as the ball is struck. An open racket face must be used on the backhand lob serve, as on the forehand. The target areas on the front wall, for either the backhand lob or hard low serve are similar to those for the equivalent serves on the forehand.

The overarm service

Occasionally players find it useful to play a hard, overarm service, rather similar to a tennis service, but without such an elaborate beginning. This serve can be of particular use to players who have extreme difficulty in serving well; otherwise, however, use it sparingly.

The screw service

This is very much an advanced variation used mainly in the men's game. The service is played from the left-hand box, as a forehand drive, the ball being aimed to hit the left-hand front corner high up the wall to 'screw' back and land in the opposite back quarter. The ball must be struck hard and with plenty of lift. It must not hit the sidewall first as this would be 'hand out'. (See Chapter 7 on the rules of the game.)

The return of service

You sometimes hear the saying 'a player is only as good as his weakest shot', meaning that a strong opponent will always exploit a player's weaker strokes to the full. This is particularly true on the return of service. Remember that in squash only 'hand in' scores points. Therefore, it is essential for the receiver of the service, 'hand out', to play the safest but most effective return available, with the object of taking the initiative away from the server. So often, by attacking on a difficult service, the receiver forces himself into making an error, when a slightly less ambitious return would at least have kept the ball in play.

The following points may help you on your return of service. First, let us look at the simple, basic return to the front wall of the court, preferably away from the centre 'T'. (Many very good services cannot be returned in this way as they require the receiver to use the more advanced shots of the volley and the boast. We shall consider those in the next chapter.)

The service, as you know, has to land in 'hand out's' back quarter of the court. So, if you are the receiver, make your opponent feel your presence in that back quarter. Take up a position approximately 30cm (12ins) away from the corner of the service box, with your shoulders slightly sideways and the racket head held up in the ready position (Fig. 22).

Fig. 22A Receiving service from the right

Fig. 22B Receiving service from the left

Watch the server in the service box, and try to watch the ball from the moment the server puts it into play. Many players watch the front wall instead of the ball as it leaves the server's hand and they often suffer the consequences by being too late to react for the return. The more advance warning you have, the better your return will be.

Assuming that the service can be returned as a drive, try to play one of the following:

a) the straight return of service down the channel – one of the safest and most effective ways of returning the ball,

b) the cross court return of service, away from the 'T' and travelling towards the opposite back quarter (Fig. 23).

Having played either of these returns, remember that you, as the receiver, must move immediately to give your opponent the direct route to the ball.

Technically, the return of service on either forehand or backhand is exactly the same as the basic strokes considered earlier. The important points to remember are as follows:

a) Start in a good position in the back quarter, in the ready position, racket head up.

b) Watch the server.

c) You are at a disadvantage as the receiver, so you must play a sensible return to put 'hand in' under pressure, rather than making an unforced error and allowing your opponent to score the point.

d) Move immediately you have played your return, so that your opponent has a direct route to the ball (Fig. 24).

e) Move to the 'T' if you have managed to draw your opponent away from the 'T'.

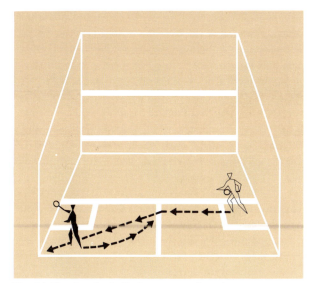

Fig. 24 Clearing the ball after return of service

Practice for the return of service
Pairs

1   With your partner, practise the service and the return of service, trying to play the shots mentioned earlier. Always think of your target area on the front wall to achieve a good length shot, whether as a straight or cross court return. Bring in some form of point system whereby the server scores if you, as 'hand out', fail to return

Fig. 23 The return of service – straight and cross court

31

the service into the prescribed areas. Avoid playing your basic return into the front of the court.

2   Progress to playing a 'normal' game, but allow one person to serve throughout. Use American scoring, whereby both players have the opportunity to score a point whether they are 'hand in' or 'hand out'.

3   As your control improves, restrict the areas in which you allow yourselves to play the ball.

Simple tactics

So far we have looked at the four basic shots – forehand drive, backhand drive, service and return of service and, before going on to the more advanced areas of the game, it is worth re-capping the simple tactical points on which you should be concentrating. You will not be able to achieve success with all these tactics immediately, but if you begin in the right way there is far more chance that as your technical game develops, so will your tactical outlook. Squash is not a game where you learn the technical skill and then progress to tactics. All these factors should be developed together to make the complete squash player. Therefore, do consider the following:

a)   Watch the ball the whole time, particularly when you are on the 'T' and the ball and your opponent are behind you in one or other back corner. If they, the ball and your opponent, are directly behind you on the 'T', then you should not be where you are.

b)   As your control improves, concentrate on playing the ball into the channels of the court, and try to keep the ball 'rolling', so that you build up confidence in your ability to rally when under pressure. Too many players 'fold' in a rally by weakly hitting the ball out or into the tin.

c)   The court is very small, particularly when you begin to appreciate that you can stay in the middle of the court and reach most shots with just two or three strides from the 'T'. So, *run for everything*. Providing you have the correct ball for the court

conditions and your standard, practically every shot should be retrieved.

d)   Have a look at your opponent during a match and see how he is coping. So often players worry too much about their own errors, their own lack of breath, when they should in fact be registering the weaker aspects of the opponent's game and his physical well-being. Your opponent may be in a far worse state than you!

e)   Use the conditioned games and practices already mentioned. They are fun, very often more energetic than a game and will help you develop that all-too-elusive control so vital in competition.

Chapter 4 **The more advanced shots**

One of the most difficult situations in squash occurs when the ball travels high in the air towards the back corners. Often the player having to cope with this shot panics, rushes to where the ball has hit the sidewall and misses it completely, occasionally breaking his racket in the process. This often happens on the return of service and in the early stages of squash a good server can sometimes win the game without so much as a rally, since the receiver has been unable to return the ball.

How then should you cope with these problem missiles from the opponent? The shots dealt with below will help you master the necessary returns.

The volley
The volley is a shot played before the ball has bounced. The ball should be struck when it is at approximately shoulder height and still high in the air, thus putting the opponent under pressure and avoiding the necessity of playing a difficult shot in the back of the court. The racket preparation should be high. A player who always has the head of the racket sweeping the floor will never be a successful volleyer and will consequently lose the opportunity to put the opponent under pressure.

The swing on the volley is similar to that for the drive, although the pathway of the racket is somewhat abbreviated. Again it is essential to concentrate on the three main stages of the swing, namely *preparation, impact, follow through*. The racket face should be slightly open as the ball is struck, to achieve the necessary height on the front wall. Concentrate on a sideways pivot of the shoulders and, if there is time, step in on the leading foot to get your weight into the shot (Fig. 25). The basic volley should be played to a length down the sidewall or deep across the court to remove the opponent from the 'T' (Fig. 26).

The teaching points are similar for both the forehand and the backhand volley, but on the **backhand volley** do concentrate on keeping the wrist firm as you prepare to play the shot (Fig. 27). Sometimes the

Fig. 25A The forehand volley – preparation

Fig. 25B The forehand volley – impact

33

Fig. 26 The volley

Fig. 27A The backhand volley – preparation

backhand volley presents problems because players allow their wrists to go loose and so only flap with the racket, instead of swinging through. The action on the volley is often likened to a *punching,* but there is far more follow through on a squash volley than when you volley in tennis.

Practice for the volley
Individual

1 One of the best ways to strengthen your forearm and improve your volley is to volley on your own against the front wall. Stand fairly close to the front wall and gently hit the ball to the wall, concentrating on keeping the racket head higher than the wrist and well extended to the side. As your control improves, gradually hit higher on the wall so that you begin to move back towards the service box and ultimately behind the service box. Then move in again towards the front wall and repeat the exercise. Progress to backhand.

The legendary Hashim Khan preparing to take a forehand volley

Fig. 27B The backhand volley – impact

2 To emphasise the importance of keeping the racket head high when volleying, stand on the 'T' and volley first a forehand and then a backhand. Start gently, otherwise you will have no time to move from one side to the other. As your control improves, try to feel your body pivoting from side to side as you alternate from forehand to backhand.

Pairs
1 Stand outside the channels of the court, one player on the short line on the forehand side and the other on the short line on the backhand side. Volley the ball to each other across the court, aiming to the centre of the front wall and above the cut line. Open your stance slightly, i.e. face the front wall a little more than for a straight shot, and take the ball well in front of you to get it across the court.
2 Progress to playing two volleys each, one as a straight shot back to yourself, then one cross court to your partner.
3 After improving control on these simple volleys, progress to the volley down the sidewall, leading up to the volley return of service. Player A should stand on the 'T', with the head of the racket up, ready to move in to play a volley. Player B should stand behind the service box and drive the ball high onto the front wall on a line with the right-hand channel. A should move in from the 'T' and volley the ball back to B. Repeat. Progress to backhand.
4 When both players have practised their volleys on both wings, progress to keeping the ball going, with the feeder at the back playing either a straight shot or a cross court shot. The volleyer on the 'T' then has to move in and play either of the feeds back to a straight length.

Practice for the volley return of service
Pairs
1 Take up the normal receiving position on the forehand side with the racket head up and watching the server. The server tries a high lob service and the receiver moves in to volley the ball, either to a straight length or as a deep cross court shot. To begin with, get the server to serve the ball away from the sidewall, as this will build up the volleyer's confidence.
2 Progress to a service which hits the front wall and then the sidewall above the service box. Now the receiver must move in and volley the ball as it comes off the sidewall. This is more difficult to set up, but it is an excellent exercise in control for the server and a very important lesson for the

receiver, so do persevere. Ideally you might ask a more experienced player to feed these returns for you. It will give him serving practice—always valuable whatever his standard.

Conditioned games for the volley

1 Condition one player to play every shot above the cut line, thus giving the other the opportunity to move in and volley these higher balls.
2 Make the volleyer move in and volley as many of the return of serves as possible, but remember that in a match you must always select the right shot at the right time, so do not volley if it really is impossible to do so.
3 Again use the conditioned game in which one player serves throughout, and make the receiver volley as many returns as possible.

The short volley

Besides the volley to a length, it is also possible to play a volley as a winning shot to the front of the court. This is a valuable shot to use when you have forced your opponent out of position and have an easy shot to deal with in the middle of the court. In this situation it is worthwhile moving in to try and volley the ball low to the front of the court, ideally so that it comes into contact with the sidewall 'nick' (Fig. 28).

The technique for the short volley is similar to that for the length, but there is less follow through, the head of the racket finishing lower in order to give a firm cut to the ball (Fig. 29). It is a more advanced volley and should be considered only when the basic volley is improving.

Caution: Players are often tempted to play this low volley as a return of service, when the opponent is in a

Fig. 28 The short volley

Fig. 29 The short volley – follow through

37

good position on the 'T'. This will only be effective if the opponent is extremely slow, not watching the ball, or the match is being played on a very cold court—so be warned and use the shot sparingly. You have a far narrower margin for error the further away you are from the front wall.

Practice for the short volley

Individual

1 From a position on the 'T', set up a lob in the middle of the court and move across and volley it to the front corner. Practise on both forehand and backhand.
2 Play a certain number of length volleys from the area near the short line, and then move in and play the low volley.

Pairs

1 Player A stands on the 'T' and player B plays a straight lob from behind the service box so that A is able to move in and volley the ball to the front corner.
2 Player A, on the 'T', chooses whether to volley to a length or to the front of the court. To be successful, a length volley must reach the area first of the service box and, later, behind the service box. Every time A fails to reach the required area, B scores a point. A scores on the number of winning volleys played to the front of the court.

The use of the sidewalls

So far we have considered only those shots which are played directly to the front wall but, of course, squash is a game where the ball may be played to any one of the four walls, providing it reaches the front wall before bouncing on the floor. So, let us have a look at the sidewalls. They are not there just for propping up the court.

On the basic drives you will have discovered that a ball which travels from the front wall towards the sidewall at an angle will come off the sidewall at the same angle. Try then to imagine for a sidewall shot

that the sidewall has become your front wall, the wall at which you are aiming. With this in mind, turn into a good position to play a basic drive to that sidewall and see what happens. If you position yourself correctly, you should find that your shot travels back towards the sidewall on the same angle as it came towards you, and, providing you strike the ball well and give it sufficient lift, your angle or boast shot should reach the opposite front corner, thus hitting three walls in all. Remember that when you strike the ball it should be on a line with your leading foot.

The angle

The term used for a shot played towards the sidewall in the front of the court is an angle. This is the shot to use when your opponent is pinned behind you and you want the ball to land in the opposite front corner, ideally just clearing the tin and landing in the sidewall nick, the crack between the sidewall and the floor (Fig. 30).

Fig. 30 The angle

The boast

The boast is another sidewall shot, but is used in the back of the court, very often as a means of returning

Rehmat Khan (Pakistan) watching the ball from the 'T' as Qamar Zaman (Pakistan) plays a boast

the ball when it is quite impossible to play a shot directly to the front wall. In this situation it is obviously a defensive shot but, if played well, it can quickly be turned into an attacking shot, when it achieves the objective of moving your opponent forwards, at full stretch, away from the 'T'. The ball may even land in the nick (Fig. 31).

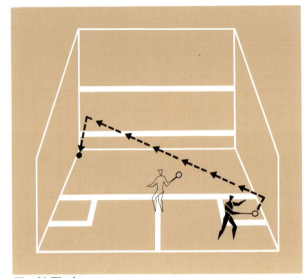

Fig. 31 The boast

The technique for the forehand or backhand boast is quite similar to that for the basic drive. The only important difference is your position in the court. A successful boast will only be achieved if you have moved correctly. Try to feel that on a squash court you are moving in a curve, to allow for the angle of the ball as it comes off the sidewall. This will give you the necessary room to play a successful shot. If the ball gets too far behind you there is no way that you will be able to return it.

As the ball travels towards the back quarter, watch it all the time, and turn so that you are facing the back corner but are well out of the channel. As the ball comes off the sidewall, move in, still facing the back corner, with the racket head up, ready to swing

through to meet the ball on a line with the leading foot. Think of the angle at which the ball is travelling towards you and play your shot back into that angle (Figs. 32 and 33). The following tips may help you in playing a successful boast:

a) Think of your stance facing the back corner. Draw an imaginary line from your shoulders to the sidewall, and this should give you the required angle for the boast.

b) Imagine a court adjacent to the one you are in and, as you play your shot to the sidewall, have the front right-hand corner of the adjacent court as an imaginary target area. Again, this will give you the correct angle.

Problems

As in all strokes, complete your swing before moving to the 'T'. Often players spoil their boast by moving during the follow through, thereby pulling the ball too far forwards on the sidewall. This results in too wide an angle and the ball then ends up in the middle of the court, at the opponent's feet. Remember, the whole point of a boast is to move your opponent forwards, away from the 'T'. After playing your stroke, you must move quickly forwards to the now empty 'T' position. If you linger at the back, you make it so much easier for your opponent to go for a winning dropshot.

Practice for the boast

Individual

In the early stages, one of the best ways of improving your boast is by using a ball on your own and playing the boast shot off your own hand feed. Practise the following on both forehand and backhand:

1   Stand on the corner of the service box, facing the back corner. Toss the ball into the service box, allow it to bounce and then step in on your left foot (right foot for the backhand), so that the ball is on a line with that foot as you strike it forwards to the sidewall.

Fig. 32 The forehand boast

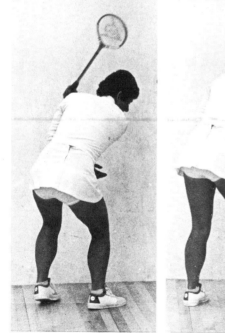   

Fig. 33 The backhand boast

Heather McKay (Australia) versus Sue Cogswell (Great Britain)

2 Progress to throwing the ball gently to the sidewall so that it comes off the wall at an angle, allow it to bounce and then hit at that same angle towards the sidewall. A ball slows up when it hits another surface, so do give your shot an adequate lift by opening the racket face.

3 If you have achieved some success, progress to feeding against the sidewall behind the service box.

Note: For a good forehand boast, the ball should first hit the sidewall, then the front wall just above the tin in the left-hand front corner, then the left-hand sidewall and finally it should come back across the floor towards the point from which it was played.

Pairs

1 Initially, get your partner to feed an easy shot to come off the sidewall near the service box. From your receiving position in the back quarter, move in and boast the return. Practise from both sidewalls.

2 As your boast improves, bring in more movement. You should always boast and then move forward to the 'T'–your shot should have removed your opponent from this central position, leaving it free for you. Progress to the following sequence: a service with server's movement to the 'T', a boast with boaster's movement to the 'T', followed by the server moving in to pick up the boast and playing a straight shot down the nearest sidewall. When kept going as a rally, this exercise brings in practice for the boast played off a good length straight shot, instead of just off the angle from the sidewall. *Co-operation* should be the key word when doing these exercises, as this will help improve your control. The boast/straight shot exercise is one of the most frequently used and most rewarding practices, and as you get better you should find it a very energetic one.

Problems

You may discover a tendency to overshoot both the boast and the straight shot from the boast when you are in a fast exchange. Try not to let yourself be rushed. Keep out in the centre of the court, economising on your movement, and you will soon find you have sufficient space to move in and boast successfully.

Conditioned games for the boast

1 Many of the exercises already described can be developed into conditioned games. Using the service, boast and length exercise, restrict one player to playing the length shots throughout the rally, while the opponent plays the boasts.

2 Again, bring in more variety as your control improves, and allow the person in front to play a cross court shot to a length as well as the straight shot, and even a short shot, to ensure that the boaster is still moving forwards to the 'T'. If you are the person in front, remember to watch the ball the whole time.

The deep back corner boast

No doubt you have discovered that, while you are able to boast the ball out of the back corner when it bounces in the area behind the service box, it seems quite impossible to cope with a ball that moves across the walls of the back corner, landing a short distance from the back wall, or, worse still, which dies in the back corner. Despair not! That need not be the end of the rally. It *is* possible to get such shots back, but it will need a little practice and a little thought on your movement in the back corner.

First, let us look at the ball which dies. If this happens only occasionally, your opponent is probably playing an excellent shot, which, during a five game match, you might expect. However, if it happens all the time, you may be playing with a ball which is far too slow and cold for your standard and the temperature of the court. If this is not the case either, then you were wrong to let the ball get where it is. You should have moved in and volleyed when it was still high and safe in the air.

43

The warning signs of a really difficult shot are often there almost as soon as the opponent starts to play a high lob towards the back corner. In this situation don't delay. Move in and volley confidently, preferably before the ball reaches the sidewall, but sometimes as it comes off the sidewall. This is not an easy volley to play, but it is better than allowing the 'death' in the back corner, so be positive.

Surprisingly, not all these high lob shots do die in the back of the court. They often travel round the back corner and bounce off the back wall in a good position for the boaster to play a successful shot. However, very often the player about to boast is by this time practically climbing up the back wall with no hope whatsoever of being able to swing the racket. This is where good movement in the back of the court proves so important.

Always watch the ball as it travels round the back corner, and as the ball moves you should move too, turning your body away from the front wall to face the back corner. It is essential that you keep the moving

ball well to the side of you, so keep well out and away from the corner. For a very deep back corner boast, a player may be as far out as the half court line as he shapes up to play the shot (Fig. 34). The basic technical points are much the same as for the easier boast higher up the court, but do remember to keep the ball well to the side of you, give yourself room to swing, open the racket face to give the ball lift and concentrate on the follow through. You will never play a successful boast if you use only half your swing.

Practice for the deep back corner boast

Individual

1   Again, valuable practice can be gained by using the self feed. Stand in the back quarter of the court and throw the ball to the back wall, aiming quite high on the wall, then move quickly, with a chassé movement to the side, in order to keep the ball well to the side of you, and boast the ball towards the sidewall.

2   Progress to a hand feed which travels across the back corner, from the back wall to the sidewall. Again, use the chassé movement to the side to boast the ball.

3   Finally, progress to a feed from the sidewall across to the backwall. As your boast improves, make it more difficult for yourself, so that you have to speed up the chassé movement.

The hand feed may present problems, particularly on the backhand, but persevere, or persuade your partner to feed for you (see below).

Pairs

1   The feeder, player A, stands in the back corner, facing the boaster, B, and tosses the ball high into the air so it bounces behind the service box. Player B then moves in to strike the ball (Fig. 35). Vary the hand feed to bring in more demanding boasts. The player boasting may begin by facing the feeder in the back corner, but should progress to moving from the 'T' position. With these

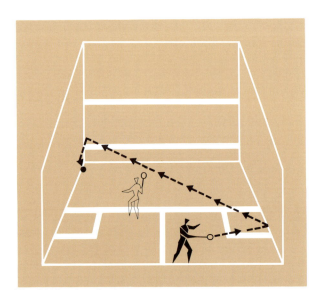

Fig. 34 The deep back corner boast

Fig. 35 Hand feeding for the boast

slower feeds you should concentrate on a good pattern of movement to and from the shot.

2 Progress to practising the boast off a racket feed. Player A stands a little in front of the left-hand service box and hits the ball high onto the front wall slightly to the right of centre. This will bring the feed deep into the back corner for B to boast. Practise on both forehand and backhand and then go on to playing a rally. A plays straight, high feeds for B to boast first on one side, then the other. This is as good an exercise for the feeder as for the boaster and will improve accuracy.

Advanced practice for the boast
Pairs

Once the boast has been mastered, there are many sequence exercises which players can use to build up their consistency and control. Try some of the following:

1 Player A self feeds for the boast and boasts from the forehand back corner, while player B prepares to move in from the 'T' and play a straight shot off the boast. The sequence continues, A boasting, B playing to a length.

2 A begins with a boast, B plays a deep cross court shot, A plays a boast and B another cross court. The sequence continues. Practise on both forehand and backhand.

3 A begins with a boast, B plays a cross court shot, A now plays a straight length shot, B plays a length shot, A boasts. Repeat.

4 A begins with a boast, B plays a cross court shot, A plays a straight shot, B plays a straight shot, A plays another straight shot and B then boasts. Repeat. This exercise now brings in boasting practice for both A and B as well as considerable movement.

5 The players are restricted to using only one back quarter of the court and the diagonally opposite front quarter. A serves the ball, B chooses whether to play a length return or a boast return, and A responds either with another length, a boast or a deep cross court shot depending on the shot B selected. The rally continues. In this way, the players are restricted to using a certain area of the court and to playing certain types of shot, but may select when to use these shots.

6 The same exercise can be used with the players also being allowed to play a straight short shot in the front quarter, when desirable.

7 As the shots improve, try to reduce the area used in the diagonal, so that eventually the target areas are behind the service box and in the opposite channel in the very front quarter of the court.

8 Develop these exercises so that the players may choose to play either a cross court shot to the opposite diagonal or a straight shot down the nearest channel. The game should now be played entirely in the channels of the court.

Note: In all these conditioned practices, start simply and increase the variations as your control improves. To add interest, play the exercises as a form

45

Geoff Hunt (Australia) under pressure but still with perfect balance and footwork

John Easter (Great Britain) in a situation where the 'wrong' foot becomes correct

of conditioned game, scoring points as the rally is either won or lost. Always try to finish with a proper game, but use the shots you have been practising whenever possible.

The volley boast

This is a shot which can be used when you have to cope with a high lob which might present problems if it dropped in the back of the court. It can also be played when you wish to pressurise your opponent by giving him less time than usual to get back into position.

Technically, the stroke is, as it sounds, a combination of the volley and the boast. As for a normal volley, the ball should be struck when it is at shoulder height, but the player should be in the position for the boast, that is with the body facing the back corner to give the required angle on the sidewall.

Practice for the volley boast

Individual

Lob the ball straight down the sidewall and move across to play a volley boast.

Pairs

Use the length/boast practices already listed with the player behind moving in to play as many volley boasts as possible.

The skid boast

This is a shot used mainly only in the top game. Again it is a boast shot, but this time played as a topspin lob, aimed high to the nearest sidewall, so that it travels high to the front wall, then back over the opponent's head to land in the opposite back corner. It is definitely a shot to be used sparingly, even after much practice, but it does have the great tactical advantage of taking the opponent by surprise and moving him away from the 'T' towards the back of the court.

The back wall boast

This shot is played off the ball which appears impossible to boast in the more normal fashion. It is played high onto the back wall to land in the diagonally opposite front corner. It is a shot which should really be considered only as a last resort, a means of at least keeping the ball in play.

Practice for the back wall boast

Pairs

Player A lobs the ball to the back corner and player B plays it to rebound against the back wall, using the forehand in the left-hand corner and the backhand in the right. Use the back wall boast only if it is impossible to boast normally. Otherwise you will become lazy in your footwork. Remember, this shot is a last resort.

The lob

Having discussed the problems that arise when the ball reaches the back of the court, let us now look at the shot you should play to put the ball into that problem area. If it presents you with great difficulties, it is tactically sound to try and put your opponent in the same position. The lob is one of the shots which will do that.

It should be played as a 'lifted' drive, the ball striking the front wall as near the top boundary line as possible, then travelling slowly over your opponent's head, ideally to sink for ever in the back corner of the court.

The lob can be used to great effect when you are under considerable pressure and need time to recover to a better position. If played well, it can change your position in a rally from that of hopeless defender to confident attacker.

Technically, it is similar to the basic forehand or backhand drive, but requires a very open racket face to give the ball the required height on the front wall. As the target area is the back of the court, this height on the front wall is all-important. Lobs may be hit as either straight or cross court shots, depending on the situation in the rally, but more lobs are played across the court because there is then less danger of the ball going above the side boundary line, since it is at its highest point as it travels across the middle of the court.

The ball should be struck early, well out in front of the leading foot, with the open racket face already mentioned. You will often be lobbing off the opponent's boast and, as this is likely to be a low shot, it is essential to bend the knees when moving in to play the lob (Fig. 36A). Try to feel that you would like to keep the ball on your racket as long as possible (Fig. 36B) and concentrate on a good follow through (Fig. 36C). Listen to the sound your shot makes on the front wall. If you hear a loud 'plunk', you are hitting too hard and the ball is almost certain to go out of court or reach the back wall at full toss, only to bounce back for your opponent to return easily. A quiet, high, floating shot is your objective.

Fig. 36A

Fig. 36B

Fig. 36C

Practice for the lob

Individual

1   Stand in the right-hand back quarter of the court and hit the ball continuously back to yourself, aiming as high on the front wall as possible (Fig. 37). Use the sound of your shot as a guide. Practise on both forehand and backhand.
2   Progress to playing a short feed in the front of the court, followed by a high, slow, cross court lob. Go on to playing a lob off an angle.

Pairs

1   Player A positions himself on the 'T', while player B stands in the back quarter and sets up the ball in the front of the court. A then moves in and lobs the ball back to B.
2   Player A stands on the 'T', while player B boasts the ball from the back corner. A moves in and lobs

Fig. 37 Height required for the lob

back cross court. The sequence continues, A lobbing, B boasting.

3 Extend the previous practice so that A can choose whether to play a cross court or a straight lob.

The front of the court

The basic tactics mentioned previously have all concentrated on getting your opponent into a defensive position behind you, so that you can move to the 'T' and gain the attacking position. Once you have achieved this objective, you should begin to think about the winning shots to be played in the front of the court. There is little point putting your opponent in a defensive position and then letting him off the hook by generously playing the ball straight back to him. The dropshot or the winning 'kill' shot should now come into your repertoire.

The dropshot

A dropshot is played when you are in command in the front of the court, well balanced, with your opponent behind you. The aim of a dropshot is to play the ball low and short to the nearest front corner. Ideally the ball should hit the front wall a fraction of an inch above the tin and travel gently towards the sidewall to land in that elusive crack between wall and floor, the nick (Fig. 38).

Disguising your shot helps to make your opponent a little slower off the mark, so your preparation should look very similar to that for a basic drive. It is only when you bring your racket forwards to the point of impact that you slow down the racket head to guide the ball to the target area. Be firm but gentle as you strike the ball. A successful dropshot requires good control of the racket head. Often, by becoming too tense and stiff in the wrist, players push at the shot and play the ball too high. There should be little follow through, the racket head ending up pointing where the shot has been aimed. The sideways stance is again similar to that for the basic drives (Figs. 39 and 40). Be careful not to fall into the trap of playing a winning

Fig. 38 The dropshot

dropshot and then failing to move out of the way, thereby obstructing your opponent and putting yourself in the likely position of getting a penalty point. After playing a dropshot to the front corner, you must move out and away to the middle of the court, and then back towards the 'T'. If you move straight back on the line of your shot you will back straight into your opponent. If you make no movement at all, you are obviously in the wrong.

The cross court dropshot and the angled dropshot

The straight dropshot is the one to be used most of the time. However, there are variations, namely the cross court dropshot, which ends up in the opposite corner, again to 'nick' in the sidewall crack, and the angled dropshot, played to the nearest sidewall and then the front wall (Figs. 41 and 42). These should be used sparingly, since they involve putting the ball across the centre of the court, rather than into the safer area of the near corner, away from the opponent. However, they are well worth considering, particularly if your opponent is reading your straight drop successfully.

51

Fig. 39A The forehand dropshot – preparation

Fig. 39B The forehand dropshot – impact

Fig. 40A The backhand dropshot – preparation   Fig. 40B The backhand dropshot – impact

Fig. 41 The cross court dropshot

Fig. 42 The angled dropshot

The heat of the court will affect the success rate of your dropshots. On a cold court it is likely that a correctly played dropshot will be a winner nearly every time. On a hot court, a winning shot is far more elusive, as a quick opponent should be able to reach most dropshots, unless he is very much out of position at the back of the court, or unless the ball 'nicks'. Nevertheless, continue to use the dropshot sensibly even on hot courts; although your opponent may reach the ball, he will have a considerable move forwards, which should begin to take its toll over a period of five games. Finally, take a tip from Heather McKay and listen for your opponent when you are shaping up to play a dropshot. If you hear his fairy footsteps close behind you, beware, and hoist the ball back whence it came to wait for another opportunity.

Practice for the dropshot
Individual
> Set the ball up for yourself in the front of the court and move in to play a dropshot. Practise both forehand and backhand and, once you have mastered the basic drop, progress to the variations.

Pairs
1   Set up shots for each other to drop, progressing to an exercise combining length, boast, dropshot, etc.
2   Play a conditioned game in which one player is restricted to playing winners in the front of the court only, when in the front area. Whilst it is possible to play a dropshot from the back of the court, it is an extremely risky shot which lets players down far more often than they care to believe. The further away you are from the front wall, the more difficult it is for you to hit the wall just above the tin.

The crash kill
As its name implies, this is a far more aggressive shot than the dropshot, but it can often be used in the

same situation in a rally, when your opponent has been forced to play a poor boast or a short ball into the front of the court.

Only consider this shot when you are in an extremely dynamic attacking position, able to move in quickly and take the ball early as it rises to the top of its bounce. Bring the racket head through firmly, cutting the ball to keep the shot low. Again, the required target area is just above the tin, as near the corner as possible, so that the ball 'nicks' about a metre from the front wall (Fig 43). The shot can be used either straight or cross court. Good footwork and balance throughout are essential.

The practices outlined for the dropshot can also be used for the crash kill.

The reverse angle

This is a shot which can be used to great effect either as a surprise return of service or as a means of coping with a loose ball from your opponent which has ended up in the middle of the court. The shot is played to the sidewall furthest away from you, about a metre from the front wall. It then bounces off that sidewall to travel almost parallel to the front wall and touch the front wall in the front corner (Fig. 44). It is most effectively used when your opponent is behind you and on the opposite half of the court.

When playing the reverse angle, concentrate on taking the ball early and angle your feet and shoulders towards the target area on the sidewall. Remember this is a shot to use when you are in an attacking position after your opponent has played a weak shot.

Practice for the reverse angle

Individual

Set the ball up for yourself in the middle of the court and play a reverse angle off it. To develop this exercise, move in and play a dropshot or a straight kill off your reverse angle.

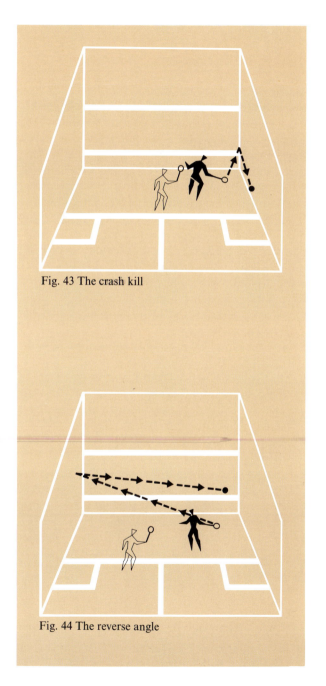

Fig. 43 The crash kill

Fig. 44 The reverse angle

Pairs

One player sets up the ball in the middle of the court and the other plays a reverse angle.

Conclusion

We have now studied in detail the armoury of strokes you will need to assemble if you are to become the complete squash player. Use the practice exercises sensibly and try to develop one new skill at a time, concentrating on your technique and movement as well as the tactical use of the shot. It is not necessary to have a coach constantly standing over you telling you what to do or where you are going wrong. Sound knowledge of the technical requirements of a particular shot will help you analyse the situation yourself and will help you improve your play during a game. If you do find a particular stroke is going wrong, use the following check-list to help you correct it.

1   Are you watching the ball *all the time*, particularly when it is behind you?
2   Is your racket in a good ready position, or is the racket head sweeping the floor?
3   Are you moving well between shots in a form of 'perpetual motion', or are you hitting, standing and then running, often too late, after you have seen the shot your opponent has played?
4   When playing your stroke are you in a good sideways position?
5   Are you stepping into your shot, striking the ball on a line with your leading knee, a comfortable distance to the side of you, or do you overrun, ending up far too near to the ball?
6   Whilst striking the ball, do you keep your balance throughout the stroke, or do you pull the shot off course by moving your body round as you hit?
7   Do you recover well to the 'T', or are you slow in recovering to a good position after playing the ball?
8   Are you thinking of where you want the ball to go *in relation to your opponent's weakness,* or are you just hitting and running?

9   Do you find you are far too close to the sidewalls?
10 Is it the ball which is in the centre of the court and not you?

If the answer is 'yes' to the majority of these questions, go back to some of the practice exercises and conditioned games in order to give yourself more time to think about what you should be doing on the court.

One of the most rewarding aspects of squash is that you can almost feel yourself improving. However, as in all sports, progress does not necessarily follow a steady ascending line on the graph of improvement— rather, it moves in fits and starts, sometimes with a tremendous leap forwards, followed by a reaction phase with, possibly, a move backwards. Expect this, take the rough with the smooth and, whether winning or losing matches, always learn from your battles to fight again another day.

Chapter 5 Tactics and match preparation

We have looked in some detail at the technical requirements for a squash player, but now let us consider further the other factors which affect performance in match play.

Good match preparation should be considered by players of all levels, no matter how light-hearted the competition. If you lose a match because your shoes are rubbing, it is entirely your own fault and, although it may provide you with an excuse in the bar afterwards, your loss will still stand as a match result.

Pre-match planning in the long term

Fitness

A majority of players obviously use their squash as a means of keeping fit. However, you will find as you move into the higher realms of competitive play—club internal leagues, club matches, championships, etc.—that you require a higher level of fitness than was previously necessary. You are now joining the ranks of those players who have to keep fit to play squash. Why allow yourself to lose a match, not because your opponent was a better exponent of the game but because you ran out of steam?

Training for squash should now begin. Fitness is not something which can be achieved in a matter of a few days. The longer and slower your build-up in training the greater your stamina will become. Any training undertaken must be done at regular intervals. Little and often is far better than a knock-out bout once a fortnight.

Most training schedules are based on a twelve week period: the first four weeks concentrating on a sound base of overall stamina, the second four weeks on improving speed and strength, and the third four concentrating more on hard practice games and keeping up the level of fitness already attained. Remember that most games of squash last no more than approximately forty-five minutes and the majority of rallies last no more than forty to fifty seconds. It is sensible, therefore, to make your overall exercise period about the length of a normal match and to base your work schedule on the length of a normal rally.

Stamina, speed and *strength* are the physical requirements for a fit squash player. Stamina can be improved by running, either jogging or, better still, interval running, that is dividing the run into jogging and sprinting. Start with a short five minute run and gradually increase both the time and the distance as your fitness improves.

Speed can be increased by sprint running in a smaller area, either in quick shuttle runs to the four corners of the court or in straight bursts (Fig. 45).

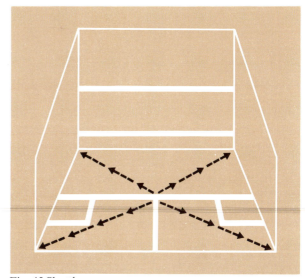

Fig. 45 Shuttle runs

Count the number of shuttle runs you can manage in forty seconds, take a ten second rest, then repeat two or three times. Again, as your fitness improves, gradually increase the number of circuits you do. Skipping with a rope, preferably a leather one, will also improve your speed and footwork. Again, skip for a set time and increase the number of skips you do as you improve.

Strength can be built up by following a sensibly planned exercise circuit, again working to a set time and repeating, trying to improve on the number of repetitions in each circuit. Under careful and expert guidance the use of light-weight training might be considered, although a well planned circuit of exercises designed to strengthen all the muscles used in squash should stand you in good stead. Remember that much of the movement in squash requires a sharp sprint start so you need to have strength in the legs and thighs.

Practice games and court work

Together with long term fitness training you should aim at a sensible build-up to successful competitive play by the use of practice games, as well as more specific coaching and general court work. Use the practice exercises and sequences already given to improve your control on all the shots, and, when planning practice games, choose your opponents carefully. Don't listen to people who tell you the only way to improve is to play players who are better than you. If you do this, you will always be in a defensive position behind the opponent and, although this may help your defensive game, it is essential to learn to play successfully when on the attack. So, on occasions, arrange an easy game with someone you think you can beat. This will boost your confidence and give you the opportunity to play those all-important attacking shots in the front of the court. It is encouraging to see the front wall with a clear view and not always through or around a stronger opponent.

If you do play with someone who is much better than you, use their better control to help you keep the ball going in longer rallies, which are so necessary when you are trying to improve your basic game. Beware of being lulled into a false sense of security – your opponent may sometimes deliberately refrain from playing a winning shot, in order to keep you running.

Be sensible about the number of games you play. Everyone, no matter what their standard, gets stale and jaded if they play too much squash, so limit yourself to two or three good games a week and use the other days to improve your overall fitness off the court, or on the court by court training and practice. The squash fanatic will often report with relish that he has played seven games in five days, but a more balanced approach to match play, practice and off-court training will stand you in better stead.

The practicalities of pre-match planning

Sleep

A well rested player is a more energetic player, so don't burn the candle at both ends. It will begin to tell in that fifth game.

Diet

Your fuel provides the energy so necessary for a hard match. So, eat sensibly, and remember that it can take up to four hours to digest a normal meal, so it is unwise to go on court just after eating—it will only slow you up.

Equipment

Check your equipment before travelling to the match, ensuring you have all that is needed – plasters, hair band, resin pads, glucose, etc. and that your clothes, socks, shoes and racket are all in a good state of repair. Never wear new shoes or clothing in a match—break them in first in a practice game so you know they will be comfortable. Look at your racket carefully for signs of worn stringing, cracked frame or old towel handle.

Travel and time of match

All too often teams arrive at their match venue some five minutes after the scheduled time, full of apologies, blaming the traffic and the difficulty in finding the courts. Don't get into this habit yourself. Check on the travel directions before you leave for the match and allow a reasonable amount of time to get there. You will do much for your own peace of mind if you arrive unruffled and in good time, with ten minutes or so to spare before the match is due to begin. At a high level of play it is advisable to arrive at least forty-five to sixty minutes before your match is scheduled and in the top echelons of the game you have to find out who is refereeing your match at least an hour before you are due to go on court. You may ask for the referee to be changed, if you wish.

The court

On arriving at a strange club the first thing you should do is inspect the court. Although all squash courts are fundamentally the same, they do have a large number of individualities which will play an important part in your tactical plan for the match.

The temperature of the court

This is one of the most important things you should note. If it is warm, you must be ready for a far bouncier ball and longer rallies. If cold, a lower, shorter game should be played, with more use of the dropshot.

The height of the court

Court ceilings vary considerably. Notice whether it is an old court, with low beams, as this will affect your use of the lob. Some courts have very dark ceilings, whether high or low, and this may affect your sighting of the ball.

Court lights

Again, these vary tremendously – in strength, height and positioning. Most new courts have fluorescent tubes, but there are still many of the large globe type of lights around. Look for any faulty lights, flickering tubes, poorly positioned lights, etc. These may all affect your sighting of the ball.

The floor

Notice the colour of the floor, whether it is light or dark, and the amount of varnish it has on it. The best floors are those with very little varnish and these will look almost white in colour. Slide your feet along and test how slippery it is. Check for loose floor boards and for large spaces in the nick area between the floor and sidewalls. Slippery floors are a menace and may affect your movement around the court.

The walls

Rub your hand along the walls of the court to check that they are not damp or sweating. Wet walls will have an alarming effect on the ball, particularly on angle or boast shots, which will tend to ricochet off the walls at most unexpected angles. If you feel that the walls are sweating, try to play an entirely straight game, avoiding the use of the sidewalls except in emergency. *Don't* tell your opponent how slippery the walls are. Let him find out for himself.

The glass back wall

Nowadays there are far more glass back wall courts around than there used to be, and these do present difficulties if you have never played in one before. Firstly, you may feel somewhat self-conscious and, secondly, because your guidelines in the back corners will appear unfamiliar, you may find yourself far too close to the glass. Don't worry about breaking it— it is unbreakable—but to help your boasts take extra care to keep well away from the walls. You may also get a reflection of yourself as you move in to play your shot. Don't be put off. Just keep your eye on the ball.

The door

Usually the door of a squash court is in the middle of the back wall. However, you will occasionally come across a door in one of the back corners, and it is surprising how this can affect your feeling for the court and, more practically, your boast out of the back corner. The ball is still in play if it hits the crack by the door, so watch the ball especially carefully in case this happens.

Sound-proofing

Courts in large sports centres and clubs in built-up areas in towns often have sound-proofing. This tends

59

to deaden the sound a shot makes as it hits the front wall and often causes players to over-hit, as they expect to hear a louder noise. Don't allow yourself to over-hit.

The opponent

The more knowledge you can glean about your opponent before the match begins the better you will be able to plan for the match. You may have played him before and this should certainly make your task easier. Ask yourself some of these more obvious questions:

1 Is your opponent left-handed?
2 What is his physical type?
3 Does he look fast or slow?
4 Is he short or tall?
5 Does he wear glasses?
6 Does he appear confident in the changing room?
7 Is he wearing any bandages?
8 Does he look very 'professional', with spare rackets, gleaming kit, etc?
9 Does he come from a hot or cold court club?
10 Do you have any details of his past match form in the way of results against other players?

Your plan of campaign

The knock-up

Use the five minute knock-up sensibly. It is not just for warming up the ball and yourself. Limber up and warm up before you go on court and you can then use the five minute period to practise your shots and to look at your opponent. Start out as you mean to go on and be as consistent as possible in the knock-up. Concentrate hard on what you are doing, the moment you start hitting. Avoid hitting the ball into the tin.

The value of length

Remember that your length shots down the sidewall are all-important, so try to get these working well at the beginning of the game.

Don't take unnecessary risks by going for difficult winning shots in the early stages of a match, when perhaps your eye is not quite in. When you are a little nervous and tense it is quite easy to miss even the most obvious shots, so play yourself in before going for the 'touch' winners.

At the start of a match, try and have a fairly long rally to see how well your opponent moves about the court, to find out whether he knows the correct way to clear a ball and whether he has a large or dangerous swing, which may give you problems if you get too close to him. Also use an early, long rally to test your opponent's fitness. It is very reassuring if he puffs and blows in the first game and often means that you will gain a few points, just through his lack of breath. Make sure you are not the one puffing and blowing!

The service

The early stages of a match are sometimes of the utmost importance. Once in the 'hand in' position, try not to throw away your advantage by immediately serving your hand out. Take your time preparing to serve and concentrate hard on putting your opponent under as much pressure as you can. As 'hand in' you have the advantage of being able to score a point if you win the rally – 'hand out' is only playing for the right to serve – so play confidently and aggressively, remembering that as the server you should have first bite at the attacking position on the 'T'.

The return of service

As receiver you are obviously in a more defensive position and it is essential to stop your opponent from scoring a point. Try to play an effective, but safe, return of service, and don't put yourself under pressure by attacking on the wrong ball. If you are receiving all the time, you must be losing, so play especially safely and avoid taking unnecessary risks. Even if you *are* losing, make your opponent work hard to win every rally.

The art of disguise

One of the most effective tactics in squash is the ability to deceive your opponent by playing a shot he is not expecting. This is why a technically unorthodox player is often very successful in match play; he will play an unusual shot which through its element of surprise becomes doubly effective. So, try not to be too predictable in your stroke selection. If your stroke technique is good, your preparation for one shot should look much the same as for another, whether you are about to hit a hard drive or a subtle dropshot. This will keep your opponent guessing for that valuable extra second and may make all the difference between a winning shot and one which he is able to return.

Crises during the match

You may have heard the saying 'never change a winning game'. If you have won the first game comfortably, it is indeed wise to keep to the same strategy. Try not to become over-confident and careless, as the lead can so easily slip away. If you have lost the first game, you should ask yourself the following questions:

a) Where were you making most of your errors?

b) Was your opponent playing many winning shots and, if so, where?

c) Why was your opponent in a position to attack?

d) Were you putting your opponent in an attacking position through your bad play, or was he there through his good play?

e) What sort of state is your opponent in? Does he appear to be tiring or does he look fit and confident?

Try to tighten up your game in the areas where you are losing points. Players often over-motivate themselves in a match by saying simply 'I must win' rather than asking 'how can I win?' A positive, practical approach to competitive play is far more rewarding than wishful thinking.

The interval between games

You are entitled to a minute's rest between games, and two minutes' rest between the fourth and fifth games, so use these pauses. Even if you have won a game very easily, it is worthwhile taking a short break, as it gives you time to collect your thoughts, as well as your breath. Some players do not like leaving the court between games, as going from the light of the court to the darkness outside can affect the eyes. It is wise, if you do go outside, to return very promptly so that you have time to readjust to the court lighting.

Broken ball

Try not to let this upset you. It is something which does occur sometimes at the most inopportune moments but concentrate hard and try to win the first rally after play is resumed.

Controversial decisions

There will always be occasions when players disagree with either a call from the marker or a decision from the referee. First of all, read Chapter 7 on the rules of the game carefully so that you know your rights as a player. It is silly to get annoyed over something on which you could have appealed, but failed to. Finally, remember that the more you *concentrate* on the game itself, the less likely you are to be ruffled by decisions from the referee. It is often the player with poor concentration who looks for a reason for losing outside himself, rather than facing up to the realities of the game.

'Set two' or 'no set'

When a game reaches eight all it is possible for both players to feel they have a good chance of winning that game. Normally, the receiver at eight all will choose to set for two, although as a surprise measure it is sometimes worth selecting 'no set'. Often the player who has fought back to eight all relaxes when he has reached that score, and allows the other player to go on and win the game. Concentrate on winning one point at a time; too much awareness of the score tends to make players over-tense.

The fifth game

This is similar to the eight all situation in that both players are in the same position with all to play for. Again, concentration, determination and a sensible approach are essential. Try to cut out your own unforced errors and keep the pressure on your opponent. Play aggressively – players sometimes over-defend when they should be on the attack. Remember matches have to be won. Your opponent will seldom concede willingly.

Match summing-up

It is possible to learn from every match, whether won or lost, provided the outcome is analysed carefully. Think about your good and bad points, the shots that let you down, your fitness, or your inability to cope with an opponent who had a difficult swing or poor movement when clearing the ball. All these points are useful ones to remember and should help you when you encounter similar conditions in the future. It is easy to say you lost because your opponent was too good or because you played badly, but this does not really give you a very helpful picture of the match. Keep asking yourself *why* you lost and what you should have done about it.

At a very high level of play, a form of match analysis is used to record the success and failure rate of a player's shots. Try asking someone in your team to 'observe' your match. It is often easier to see from the gallery where a player is going wrong and a helpful word from a team member between games can be of great benefit.

The following forms of match analysis may help when observing another player's game, and can be used by a coach or team captain when watching a match.

Simple analysis of the basic strokes

Try to record every shot the player makes during a rally using plus and minus signs to indicate the success or failure of each type of shot. If he plays a poor cross court shot (width) and the opponent hits a winner off

that shot, then a minus (−) would be recorded on the sheet. In the analysis below it is quite apparent that the player under analysis is far weaker on the backhand side than on the forehand and is playing far too many shots across the court.

| Length | Forehand | + + + + − |
| | Backhand | − − − + − |

| Width | Forehand | − + + + + − + + − + |
| | Backhand | − − − + − + − − + − |

| Service | Right box | + + + + − |
| | Left box | − − − − − |

| Return | Forehand | + + + + − |
| | Backhand | − − − − − − |

A more advanced form of match analysis may be used for better players. In this system you are looking at the shots played to and from certain areas on the court.

Attacking game in the front of the court

| Straight winning kills | Forehand | + + + + + + |
| | Backhand | − + |

| Cross court winning kills | Forehand | |
| | Backhand | − |

| Straight dropshots | Forehand | + + − |
| | Backhand | |

| Cross court dropshots | Forehand | |
| | Backhand | |

| Angles | Forehand | |
| | Backhand | |

It is particularly interesting to know where an opponent plays a winning shot when in this attacking position in the front of the court. From the analysis above it is obvious that the player has a marked preference for hard straight kills on the forehand and plays very little else. Most of us have favourite winning shots and if you are able to read your opponent's most effective winner you have immediately neutralised its greatest strength.

Defensive game in the back of the court

Length	Forehand	$- - - - - + +$
	Backhand	$-$
Width	Forehand	
	Backhand	
Boast	Forehand	$+ + + + +$
	Backhand	$-$
Lob	Forehand	
	Backhand	

From this analysis it is apparent that the player has a strong forehand boast but not very much else.

It is also interesting to do a match analysis linked to the score. Players often suffer bouts of lost concentration at similar moments in each of their matches. Notice how often a player reaches a position of advantage in a game, for example 7 – 5, and then goes on to lose the next five rallies in a row. This can happen for a number of psychological reasons. Some people see themselves winning before they have in fact done so and, in thinking of the win, they let the match slip away. Other players find their maximum concentration only when they are fighting to survive. Thus it may be easier to catch up from 0 – 8, match ball, than actually to win that match ball.

For this type of match analysis a form of shorthand is needed to record the winning and losing shots. Again it is easier to observe one player at a time.

Method of shorthand:

Forehand length	FL	Backhand length	BL
width	FW	width	BW
boast	FB	boast	BB
volley	FV	volley	BV
dropshot	FD	dropshot	BD
lob	FLo	lob	BLo
angle	FA	angle	BA
kill	FK	kill	BK

Analysis linked to the score

Player A	Player B	Front court	Back court
0R		− FD	
1L		− FK	
2R			
	0R		+ BL
	1L		+ FB
	2R	+ FV	
2R		− FD	

Player B above is the one being analysed. Player A starts out by serving from the right-hand box and B returns with a poor forehand dropshot in the front of the court. A thus takes the first point and then serves from the left-hand box. B plays a poor forehand kill, A takes the second point and serves from the right. B now plays a successful backhand length and wins the service, which he takes from the right-hand box. He goes on to make two more winning shots, before serving his hand out on a poor forehand dropshot. With the score at 2 all, A serves again from the right-hand box.

Finally, remember that matches are often won on the practice court, so the more hard work you put in there, the more rewarding your progress should be when you enter the field of competitive play.

63

Chapter 6 Working as a group

Much can be gained from training in a group. Nowadays, more and more group coaching is being undertaken for players of all standards and, even at the very highest levels, players will train in a form of squad system, often working with three or four to a court.

A prerequisite of any successful group training session is that all those taking part should be *active*. This will only be achieved if the session is well planned and organised by the coach or team organiser. Here then are a number of points to consider if you are involved in the running of a group training session.

Numbers and length of session

Many of the practice excercises already mentioned can be used with more than two people on a court. The ideal number for a group session is four, although at beginner level it is quite possible to cope with five or six players per court. This means that a squad of twelve to eighteen players can be usefully organised on three courts for one to two and a half hours, according to the players' level of fitness and ability.

Standard of players

You will seldom have a group of players all of the same ability, so it is essential to assess the standard of your group and then divide it accordingly. It is advisable to put the stronger players together and, although the theme for the session will be the same for all, the work rate on each court can be different. Stronger players need to practise with more precision, tighter target areas and in more challenging situations. Beginners need less pressure in order to improve and consolidate their technical skill.

The left-hander

In a confined area the variation to the rule sometimes presents difficulties to the inexperienced coach or organiser, but it really does not matter whether you have left-handers or right-handers. Just remember to put them in a good position to practise their shots and try to keep to a 'theme' of drives or volleys, without specifying forehands and backhands. This will quite naturally give everyone practice on both wings.

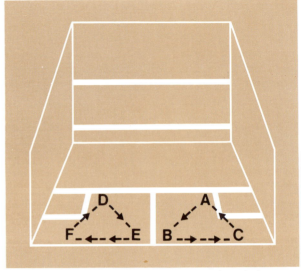

Fig. 46 Court organisation for an even number of players

Activity and use of court space

It is essential to keep the whole group active and this will only be achieved by good organisation and quick rotations. If you have six players per court, you might have two doing some form of fitness exercise while the other four are working. If you have an even number of players in your group, it is possible to divide the court into two halves, with equal numbers working on each side (Fig. 46). If you have an odd number of players, your rotation must involve the whole court to ensure that everyone has the same amount of time in each space (Fig. 47).

It is often possible to keep a group of six players active by making use of the sidewalls as a practice area. The more hitting time a player can get in a group training session the better, so always ask yourself how you can best utilise the space available and don't just assume you must have your group hitting to the front wall. Try having players A and B feeding to the left-hand sidewall for C and D to play straight shots back, while E feeds to the right-hand sidewall for F to play a straight shot (Fig. 48).

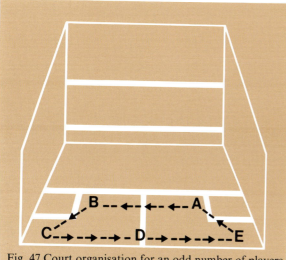

Fig. 47 Court organisation for an odd number of players

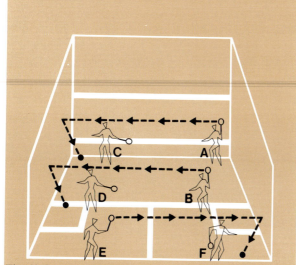

Fig. 48 Court positions for group of six using the sidewalls

If one or two players are standing out longer than the others, it is your fault as coach. You must ensure that everyone gets the same amount of practice.

Safety

This is of great importance. Players working in a group must be made aware of the dangers of flailing rackets, and of wild and exaggerated movement. In fact, the more aware they are of this, the better they will develop ball and racket control, one of the greatest assets to an up-and-coming squash player.

The ball

Try to use the correct speed of ball for the court conditions, preferably a slightly faster one than used normally in a game. Each player should have a ball. Beware of leaving balls loose on the court; they may get cold or trip people up.

Logical lesson progression

Whatever the theme of your session may be, the progressions used must be logical and within the capabilities of the group as a whole. In the early stages, you should have some form of set practice, such as hitting to a target area, and then progress to a more demanding exercise requiring more movement, extending that exercise to some form of conditioned practice or game involving two people. Finally, you should end with the game itself.

On the following pages a number of lesson progressions are shown for all the basic strokes and these may be helpful when planning your group sessions. It will keep the interest of both the players and the coach/organiser if you have a new variation to use on a set exercise. If your practice is always the same it will become dull and this lack of imagination may be reflected in the game.

The basic drives

As already mentioned, the more practice players are able to get using a ball each the better. Assuming that you have four players per court, try some of the following exercises:

65

Gogi Alauddin (Pakistan) in a controlling position against Johnny Lesley (Great Britain)

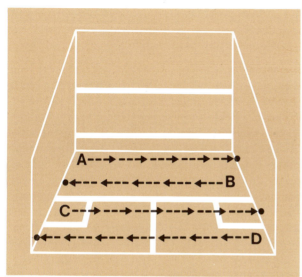

Fig. 49 Court positions for individual rallying to sidewalls

1 A warm-up session with the players rallying to the sidewalls (Fig. 49).

2 Two players rallying individually to the front wall on forehand and backhand, counting strokes which: a) hit above the cut line and bounce in the channel, b) hit above the cut line and bounce in the service box, c) hit above the cut line and bounce beyond the service box and d) hit above and below the cut line alternately, thus bringing in more movement. Players hit for sixty seconds and then change over. The two non-hitters should count the others' successful hits.

3 Progress to working in pairs, player A starting behind the service box and setting the ball up in the front of the court for player B to move in and play a length shot. Players C and D do the same on the backhand. Initially it is advisable to stop the ball after the length shot has been played, but as control improves so a set rally may develop.

4 The previous exercise can now be turned into a competitive game in which the feeder at the back tries to force the front player to play out of the required area, namely the service box. Players score up to nine points, American scoring, and then change positions.

5 To bring in movement to the 'T' after playing the length shot, it is possible to do a form of circling exercise, involving the whole group. The coach/organiser stands behind the service box and sets the ball up in the front of the court for the players to move in, in turn, to play a length shot back to the feeder, and then move to the 'T' (Fig. 50). The importance of watching the ball the whole time should be stressed.

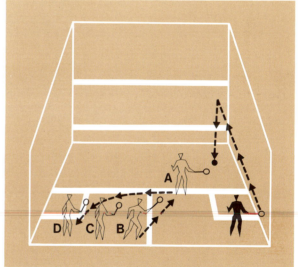

Fig. 50 Practising length shots with a feeder

6 The next progression could be, without a feeder, allowing the players to play a shot one after the other, followed by movement to the 'T'. The aim should be to set up a consistent rally using some of the target areas already mentioned (Fig. 51).

7 After this group progression it should be possible for the players to work again in pairs, but now with the movement to and from the 'T'. This will highlight the importance of clearing the ball correctly after playing a good length shot. Player

67

Fig. 51 Practising length shots without a feeder

A starts behind the service box, player B on the 'T'. Player A starts the rally, playing a length shot to the back of the service box, and then moving behind player B as he comes in to play his shot. Remember that if you start off behind your opponent, no matter how good your length shot is, you have to move round the *back* of your opponent to allow him the direct route to the ball. If you move directly forwards to the 'T' you will automatically obstruct. Players A and B should work for sixty seconds, counting the strokes in their rally, and then players C and D should take over. It is safer to have two players working and two resting, although, at a high level, both pairs can work on this exercise at the same time.

8 A further competitive element can be brought in with two players trying to beat each other in the one half of the court. The winner of the rally should then stay on and play a newcomer. If one player stays on for more than three wins, he can be 'retired', to ensure that the others have their turn.

9 A final progression would be to allow the players to play a conventional game, but with the emphasis on straight length shots.

The service

The service can be practised from one of the boxes, with the players coming in, one at a time, to serve and move to the 'T'. It is also possible to serve using both boxes; player A serving from the right, moving to the 'T' and then on to the left-hand back corner, whilst player B serves from the left, moves to the 'T' and ends up in the right-hand back corner. Players C and D then move in for their services (Fig. 52). In this way there is more activity and more serving practice. The emphasis should be on where to aim on the front wall in order to achieve the target area required in the back corners.

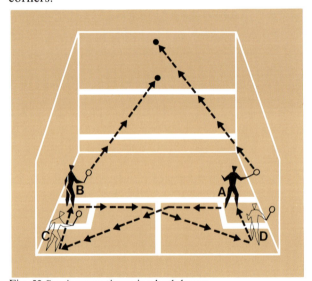

Fig. 52 Serving practice using both boxes

The return of service

Again this can be practised as a rotation exercise.

1 Player A serves, player B receives and the remainder of the group wait in the back corner behind A. Player A then moves to the receiving position and player C comes in to serve.

2 Having had some set practice on service, movement to the 'T' and return of service, it should be possible to develop this into a normal rally of straight shots between two players, using the one half of the court.

3 Finally, a conditioned game could be used in which one player serves throughout and one player receives. Every point is scored whether the rally is won by the server or the receiver and after one game to nine points they change roles.

The volley

Group practice for the volley can be very similar to that for the drive.

1 Each player has a ball and volleys individually to the sidewall.

2 Progress to volleying to the front wall with emphasis on higher and deeper volleys. One player works on the forehand, one on the backhand; the other two change in after sixty seconds.

3 Progress to practising in pairs, with players A and B on the short line moving in to volley high feeds from C and D (Fig. 53).

4 Progress to a circling exercise with the anchor/feeder setting the ball up for the players to volley in turn.

5 Progress to a circling exercise without a feeder; player A drives from the service box area and moves to the 'T', player B volleys, player C moves in and either drives or volleys, depending on the height of the previous shot, player D then moves in either to drive or volley.

6 The volley can also be practised as a return of service, the group rotating as in the return of service practice.

7 Another more advanced progression would be to use two balls with three of the players working, and the fourth waiting by the door. Player A starts out on the 'T', player B starts behind the right-hand service box with a ball and C starts behind the left-hand service box with a ball. B serves the ball straight and A moves in and volleys back to B who stops the ball. C then immediately serves and A volleys straight on the backhand back to him; C stops the ball. B then feeds again.

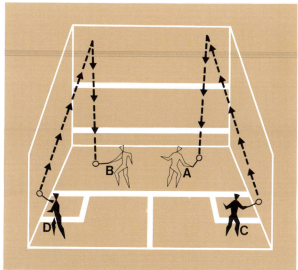

Fig. 53 Practising the volley in pairs

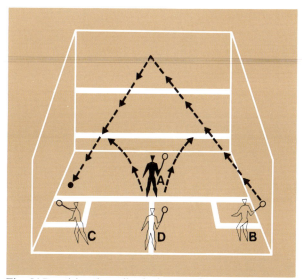

Fig. 54 Practising the volley by intercepting cross court feeds

69

Practising length shots in a group

Fig. 55A

Fig. 55B

Rhonda Thorne (Australia) in full flight on the backhand

A is thus moving from side to side to intercept these alternate feeds. After sixty seconds the players move round one position.

8   A further development could be to use one ball. Again player A starts on the 'T' and players B and C lob the ball across the court to one another with A trying to intercept as many volleys as possible. Initially A should try to play straight volleys, but may progress to cross court and straight as control improves. After sixty seconds the players move round one position (Fig. 54).

9   A conditioned game for the volley can be used whereby one player has to hit every ball above the cut line, except when boasting, thus encouraging the other player to volley as much as possible. It is unrealistic to try to volley everything.

The boast

The simple hand feeds mentioned in Chapter 4 for practising the boast can also be used in a group session, with two players working in each corner (see Fig. 35). Except on the very deep back corner boast, it is quite safe to have pairs working in each corner, though it is important to re-emphasise safety at this stage. Practices with racket feeds can be as follows:

1   The coach/organiser feeds the ball and the players come in in turn to boast and then move forwards to the 'T' (Fig. 56).

2   The players can then progress to feeding for each other. Player A on the 'T' feeds the ball for player B to boast; B then takes A's position and player C comes in to boast.

3   An exercise involving all four players can be used as follows: A plays a length shot for B to boast, C picks up this boast and plays a length backhand for D to boast.

4   It is then possible to remove one of the back players, say D, so that players A and C feed straight shots for B to boast on both sides.

5   It is also possible to do this the other way round with two players at the back of the court boasting and one player on the 'T' playing the length shots.

Fig. 55C

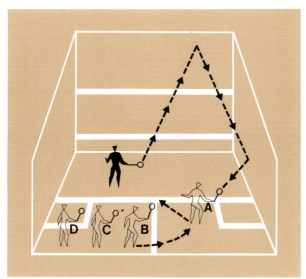

Fig. 56 Practising the boast with a feeder

6 These exercises involving four or three players can then be reduced so that two players do the length/boast practice.

7 Further exercises can be used bringing in variations in the length of shot played, e.g. a deep forehand length followed by a forehand boast, then a shorter, straight backhand, followed by a backhand boast.

8 Other variations may be used at this stage, bringing in more length shots before the boast (see Chapter 4). The deep cross court shot can be included as and when necessary.

In all exercises involving two players, the two who are waiting should stay at the back of the court and change in after approximately sixty seconds.

The dropshot

Once your group has mastered the technique of the boast, it is essential to bring in some form of exercise for the dropshot. One of the basic tactics in squash is to draw the opponent forwards, making him run, after first forcing him to the back of the court.

1 As an introductory practice, have the players working one in each corner using a ball each.

2 Progress to working in pairs, two players on the forehand side, two on the backhand. The person at the back feeds for the front player to move in and play the basic dropshot.

3 This can then be developed into an exercise involving all four players. Player A plays a length feed, player B boasts and player C plays a dropshot. Player C then starts a new rally with a straight backhand feed to player D, who plays a backhand boast; A plays the forehand dropshot. Repeat and after a time rotate one position.

4 Progress to having three players working. Player A on the 'T' plays a straight length, player B plays a boast and player C moves in from the front of the 'T' to play a dropshot. A then moves in quickly to pick up this dropshot and play the ball to a length on the backhand for B to boast. This will make C, playing the dropshot, realise the importance of moving away from his shot after playing it to the corner. Rotate after a short while, bringing in the waiting player.

5 Progress to working in a pair. Player A plays a length, player B boasts, player A plays a dropshot and player B runs in to play a length shot off the dropshot. A then runs back to boast and the sequence continues. An energetic practice!

6 Progress to practising a series of dropshots. Start the exercise with a length shot, followed by a boast, and then have a dropshot followed by a series of dropshots. This will again make the players move quickly in order to keep out of each other's way.

7 A conditioned game for the dropshot can be played, making the players use the dropshot after a boast is played. This will help the player who usually never thinks of using a dropshot.

The lob

Group practices for the lob are very similar to those

73

listed for the drive and the boast. Initial exercises should concentrate on the height and control required for the straight lob, but practice for the cross court lob should also be considered, since this is often the shot a player has to use to get himself out of trouble.

The following sequence exercises can be used for the cross court lob:

1   Player A serves, player B boasts the return of service and A moves in and lobs the ball cross court back to B to boast again. The exercise continues – lob and boast. Players A and B work for a set period and then change places with C and D, who have been waiting behind the service box on A's half of the court.

2   Player A serves, player B boasts, player A plays a dropshot and B runs in and lobs the ball cross court. A then boasts and the sequence continues – dropshot, cross court lob, boast, etc.

Fig. 57 The forehand lob – preparation and follow through

British Professional Champion Ahmed Safwat lunging low for a backhand

3 A conditioned game can be used in which both players try to use the lob as often as possible, particularly after their opponent has played a boast.

Other variations

All shots which can be practised on an individual basis can also be practised in group training. The important points for the coach/organiser to remember are those already mentioned – quick rotations, good, safe organisation, logical sequences in which the shots used and the movement required are similar to those used in the game itself. Try to use yourself as an 'anchor' to get the practices working successfully before you leave the group to work on its own. It is advisable to try out these sequences yourself before demonstrating them to your class. 'Actions speak louder than words' and a good demonstration at the start of a practice will make the sequence so much clearer and easier for your pupils to learn correctly.

Fig. 58 The backhand lob – preparation and follow through

Chapter 7 **The rules of the game and their interpretation**

A sound knowledge of the rules is a prerequisite for any successful game of squash. Squash can be, and often is, an extremely dangerous game when played by those who do not appreciate the rules on obstruction and being hit by the ball. It is also important for a player who reaches the higher, competitive stage of the game to know his rights in relationship to the marker and the referee and the exact duties of these two officials. First, however, let us look at the practical rules which will affect all players, whether they are playing with a marker and referee or just on their own in a so-called friendly game.

Time of arrival
It is important to be on time for your match. Your opponent is quite entitled to claim the contest if you are more than ten minutes late, and in fact some clubs have a rule whereby you lose the court if you are not there to play within five minutes of the scheduled booking time.

Knock-up
You are entitled to a five minute knock-up either with your opponent or, if you prefer, on your own. If you elect to knock up on your own, you should toss to see who knocks up first. The first player then has three and a half minutes and the second player two and a half minutes; the first player has longer in order to warm up the ball.

Rest between games
You are entitled to a one minute rest between games and two minutes' rest between the fourth and fifth game. Play during a game must be continuous. You may not leave the court during a game, only in the interval between games, so remember to take your sweater off before the start of a game, not during it.

The ball should be left on the floor in the rest period between games. If you wish to knock up during this period you must first obtain your opponent's permission to do so.

New ball
If the ball breaks during a match, the new ball should be knocked up by both players until they agree that it is fit for them to resume play, i.e. when the ball is sufficiently warm.

The score
A match will normally consist of the best of five games, i.e. the first player to win three games wins the match. Each game is played to nine points, except when the score reaches 8 – 8, when the receiver then chooses to play either 'set two' (playing to ten points), or 'no set' (to nine points). The game never goes beyond ten points. Women play the same number of games as men.

The toss
The players 'toss' a racket to decide who should serve first. Most squash rackets have two rows of coloured stringing, known as trebling, across the top and bottom of the strings. If you run your finger along this trebling you will feel that one side is smooth to the touch and the other is rough. Hence the call 'rough or smooth'. The winner of the toss will always serve first, as you only score a point when you are the server, known as 'hand in'. The receiver, known as 'hand out', wins only the right to serve if he wins the rally.

Points won and lost
The rally will cease when the ball is struck on or above the boundary line, or on or below the tin. The ball may not be carried or double hit on the strings of the racket, and may not touch the player as he plays the shot. The ball may be hit before it has bounced or after it has bounced once on the floor. It ceases to be in play after it has bounced twice.

Service
Each rally begins with a service. The server, 'hand in', must stand with at least one foot within the service box and must strike the ball before it touches the ground so that it hits the front wall above the cut line and lands in the opposite back quarter of the court, avoiding contact with the lines (Fig. 59). At the start of a game, or when he wins the service, the server may

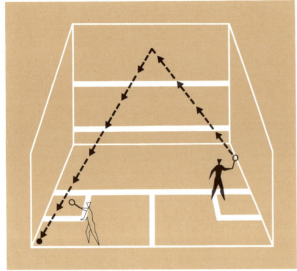

Fig. 59 A good service

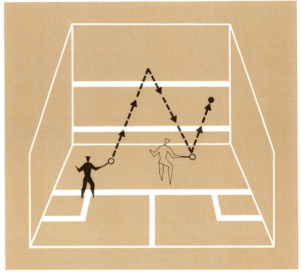

Fig. 60 'Hand out' takes a single service fault

serve from either box, but if he wins the rally his next service must be taken from the opposite box; from then on he continues to change sides until he loses a rally.

Single service faults
There are four single service faults. These are as follows:
1 a foot fault: 'hand in' must have one foot entirely within the service box; the other foot may be placed anywhere,
2 when the ball touches the cut line or hits the front wall below the cut line,
3 when the ball touches the short line or lands in front of the short line,
4 when the ball touches the half court line or lands in the server's back quarter of the court.

The receiver, 'hand out', may elect to take a single fault and if he strikes at the ball the rally is then in progress (Fig. 60). If he chooses not to take the first service fault he must make no attempt to hit the ball and 'hand in' will then take a second service. If 'hand in' serves a second single service fault, he loses the rally.

Note: Even if the receiver takes a second service fault and his return is not good, he will still be awarded the rally. Two single service faults immediately make the score 'hand out'.

Serving 'hand out'
The single service faults apart, there are a number of occasions when the server can serve his hand out in one hit. These are as follows:
1 when the ball is struck on or above the boundary line,
2 when the ball is struck on or below the tin, or on the floor,
3 when the server misses the ball completely,
4 when the ball is struck to the sidewall before the front wall (this normally occurs on a screw service – see Chapter 3),
5 when the server strikes the ball and catches it himself before or after one bounce.

A let
A 'let' is the term used when a rally has to be replayed. A let shall always be allowed in the following cases:

Philip Kenyon (Great Britain) at full stretch

1   when the ball breaks during a rally,
2   when the receiver is not ready to receive the service,
3   when the ball bounces out of court on its first bounce (a rare occurrence),
4   when the lights go out during a rally (a regular event on courts with light meters),
5   when something is dropped in the court from the gallery and distracts the players.

Lets are also allowed in cases of obstruction or players being hit by the ball (see below).

Being hit by the ball

At the higher levels of the game this should happen only rarely, although at the beginner stage players often get hit, usually because they are obstructing and their opponent nevertheless plays the stroke. It is important to know your rights if you are hit by the ball.

1   If the ball which struck you was travelling directly to the front wall, the stroke is awarded to your opponent. Sadly, you get hit *and* lose the rally (Fig. 61).

2   If the ball was travelling to or from the sidewall or from the back wall when it hit you, a let would be played, providing the ball would have reached the front wall (Fig. 62). If, in addition, it was a winning stroke which was intercepted, the stroke would be awarded to the striker (Fig. 63).

3   If the ball would not have reached the front wall, either directly or via any of the other walls, the point goes to the non-striker.

Turning on the ball

There are occasions, usually in the backhand corner, when a player will allow a hard, high, angled ball to travel round the back corner and, instead of boasting the ball out on the backhand, will follow it round and play a forehand. In this situation, because the player has turned, a let will be allowed if the ball hits the opponent, either on its direct flight to the front wall, or on its way via any of the other walls.

Note : This is one of the most dangerous situations that can arise in squash and players should make every effort to refrain from hitting their opponent with the

Fig. 61 Ball travelling directly to front wall – stroke to B

Fig. 62 Ball travelling to sidewall – let

ball. Providing the stroke could have been played a let will be allowed. You do not have to hit your opponent in order to be awarded the let!

Mentally turning

If the player has not physically turned but has just waited for the ball to travel behind him with the intention of then playing it on the forehand, the same rules will apply as for physically turning. (Mentally turning was previously considered to be different from physically turning.)

Hitting yourself with the ball

If you play a shot and the ball comes back and hits you, you will lose the rally except in the following cases:

1   If you are prevented from getting out of the line of your shot by your opponent, a let may be allowed.

2   If your opponent has shaped up to play a shot but misses it or changes his mind at the last moment, a let will be allowed, even though the ball has hit you, providing the opponent would have had a chance of hitting the ball at a second attempt (Fig. 64). If the opponent had no opportunity of a

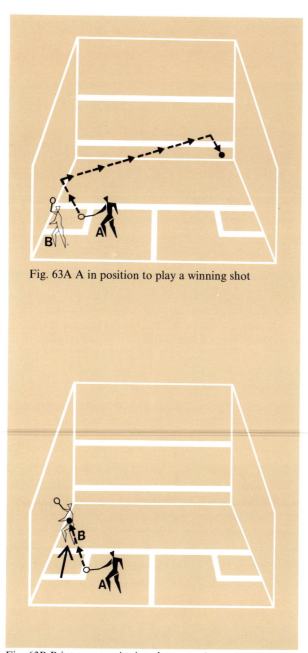

Fig. 63A A in position to play a winning shot

Fig. 63B B intercepts winning shot – stroke to A

Fig. 64 B might hit ball at second attempt – let

second attempt, the point will be awarded to you, the striker, even though the ball has come back and hit you.

3 If your opponent shapes up to play a shot (often a volley), but decides to leave it and moves back to make a second attempt at a shot and then hits you with the ball on this second attempt, a let will be allowed, providing the ball would have reached the front wall, whether as a direct or indirect hit.

Obstruction

The rules state quite clearly that 'after playing a ball, a player must make every effort to get out of his opponent's way'. So, before striking the ball, you should have had:

1 a fair view of the ball as it travelled from the front wall for you to play your shot (Fig. 65),

2 freedom to swing your racket and make your stroke in a safe arc,

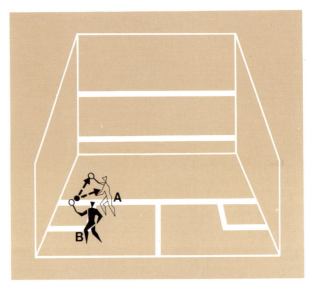

Fig. 66 A's position prevents B from playing shot to front wall – stroke to B

If you feel that your opponent has not given you any one of these three points you should refrain from hitting the ball. By *not* stopping you may well hit your opponent with the ball and, if this happens, the rules already mentioned will apply. If you do stop, the following line of thinking should help you and your opponent to come to a fair and right decision.

Remember, the rules state quite clearly that a player must make every effort to get out of the way so that the opponent can get to the ball and play his stroke. So, if the opponent has made no movement whatsoever to get out of the way, whether by design, or because he played a poor shot which immediately came straight back to him, or because he has made a poor recovery from the shot, the stroke should be awarded to you, the striker, provided you were in a position to get to the ball (Fig. 67).

What often happens, however, is that a player does make some attempt to get out of the way, but just not enough and there is still an obstruction. In this situation you must ask yourself if you were in a position to play a winning shot. If the answer is yes,

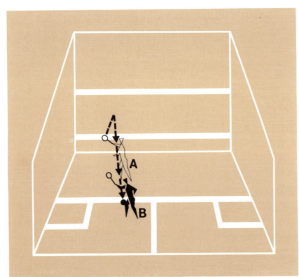

Fig. 65 A's position prevents B from seeing the ball – stroke to B

3 freedom to play your shot to anywhere on the front wall and to the sidewalls near the front wall (Fig. 66).

Fig. 67 A does not clear the ball – stroke to B

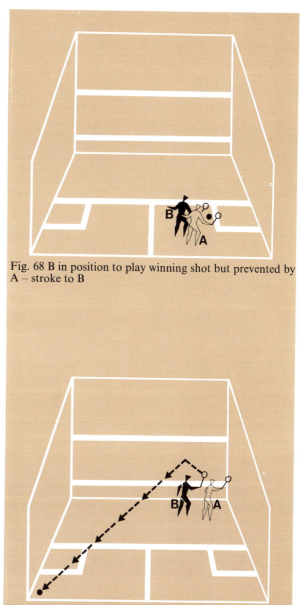

Fig. 68 B in position to play winning shot but prevented by A – stroke to B

Fig. 69 B in position to play winning shot but prevented by A – stroke to B

then the stroke should be awarded to you. If you were not in a position to play a winning shot and the opponent was making an effort to get out of the way, a let should be played. You do not have to take into consideration a player's ability to play a winning shot when coming up with this decision. It is enough that there are certain winning situations on the court when the opponent is hopelessly out of position (Figs. 68 and 69).

If you play a let when one player has had a considerable advantage over his opponent during a rally, but has been prevented from playing the final winning shot, then it is obviously unfair to put the players back on an equal level in that rally. This is why it is sometimes extremely annoying if a referee asks you to play a let ball when you had been in that position of advantage. The same applies to the situation where you might have hit your opponent with the ball. After all, if you do hit your opponent on a direct hit to the front wall it is your stroke. It is logical, therefore, that if you refrain from hitting him it should also be your stroke.

The officials

You now know how to play the game according to the rules without a marker and referee, but it is important to understand the role of these two officials and how they will affect you when you reach the level of competitive squash.

Most top level matches will have two officials, one acting as marker, the other as referee, but in many club matches it is quite usual to have one person officiating in both these roles. Even if there is only one official in the gallery, all the rights of the players concerning appeals to the referee still apply.

The role of the marker

The marker is responsible for the general organisation of the match and, although he makes no decisions on obstruction, appeals from the players, etc., a good marker can help the smooth running of the game by his competent calling of the score and correct decision making on whether the ball was in or out. It is therefore important for the marker to have good eyesight and a clear voice – he speaks to both the players and the gallery. The exact calls of the marker and their uses are given below.

$2\frac{1}{2}$ minutes – to make the players change sides half way through the knock-up.

10 seconds – to be used in the knock-up at 4 minutes 50 seconds to warn the players the match is scheduled to begin; also given during the interval between games to get the players back on court.

Time – the term used to start the game.

Stop – the term used to stop play during a rally.

Final of the British Championships – introduction to the match.

A serving, B receiving – correct introduction to the players (by name).

Best of five games – indicates the length of the match.

Love all – the call of the score at the start of the match. As soon as the score has been called the players may begin.

Foot fault – given when the server's one foot is not correctly placed in the box.

Fault – when the service is incorrect.

Out – when the ball is on or above the boundary line.

Down – when the ball hits the sidewall before the front wall on service.

Not up – when the ball hits the floor or the tin.

Double hit – when the player carries or double hits the ball.

Hand out – indicates the change of serve.

One love – the call of the score; the server's score is called first.

One love, one fault – the correct call to be used when 'hand in' is one point up and has served a single service fault, not taken by the receiver. This should be called before the second service is taken.

Game ball – to be used at 8 – 2, game ball.

Match ball – to be used at 8 – 2 when it is match ball.

8 – 8, set two – when the game has reached 8 – 8 and the receiver chooses to play to ten points.

8 – 8, no set, game ball – when the receiver chooses to play to nine points.

A leads one game to love, love all – introduction to second game.

Note: You are not allowed to commence play until the score is called. It is therefore essential to listen carefully a) to know when to begin and b) to make certain that the score called is correct.

Possible calls after an appeal to the referee

After an appeal from 'hand out', score at 6 – 2:

let ball, 6 – 2, or

no let, 7 – 2, or

stroke to B, hand out, 2 – 6.

After an appeal from 'hand in' with the score at 8 all, no set:

let ball, 8 – 8, match ball, one fault, or

no let, hand out, 8 – 8, no set, game ball, or

game to A, 9 – 8.

The role of the referee

All appeals that you make as a player go direct to the referee. You have no dialogue with the marker. The referee may often have a far less vocal time than the marker but he does have the more difficult role, since he has to give a fair decision when an appeal is made. It is therefore essential that the referee has a good knowledge of the rules of the game and a sound interpretation of these rules.

The powers of the referee

The referee must ensure that there is fair play on the court. If, in his opinion, one player is infringing the rules, he may stop play and award either a let or a stroke, depending on the situation. Once the referee has made a decision there can be no further appeal from either player. If you try to argue, you can be cautioned for time wasting. In addition to answering appeals from the players, the referee checks the marker, so he must also record the score. Because his decision is final, the referee should use his supreme power wisely and only stop play in exceptional circumstances, for example in the case of danger or when the marker makes an obvious error.

When to appeal to the referee

If the marker makes no call, or you are unhappy with his call, or feel that he should have called a ball out or not up, you should appeal to the referee at the end of the rally. If he agrees with your appeal you will either be awarded the rally or a let will be played, depending on the situation. If there is doubt in the referee's mind, it is obviously fair to play a let.

If the score is called incorrectly you should appeal before the next rally begins.

As 'hand in' you may appeal if the marker calls fault to your second service. You may not appeal on the call of fault/foot fault on the first service.

As 'hand out', if the marker fails to call fault on the *first* service and you feel it was a fault, *you must not return the service.* If you do take the service you give up the right of appeal. If the marker fails to call fault on the *second* service, you may take the service and even if you then lose the rally, you may still appeal to the referee that the second service was a fault. If the referee is uncertain a let will be played. If the marker makes a late call of fault you are entitled to appeal to

the referee on the grounds that the late call put you off. If the referee feels this is correct a let will be played. If you are not ready to receive the service, you should make no attempt to hit the ball, whether it is a fault or not, and a let will be played, provided that you were not time wasting.

An appeal on the grounds of obstruction by the opponent should be made at the time of the obstruction. If you feel you have not had a fair view of the ball, or freedom to swing your racket to play your stroke, or freedom to play your shot to where you want on the front wall or on the sidewall near the front wall, you should *stop* and appeal to the referee. This also applies to the occasion when your opponent accidentally steps on your foot or knocks into you during a rally.

Referee's possible decisions when interference occurs

a) Deliberate obstruction or total lack of effort to get out of the opponent's way – stroke to obstructed player.
b) Opponent prevented from playing a winning shot – stroke to obstructed player.
c) Obstruction, but opponent not in a winning position – let ball.
d) Potential obstruction, but opponent not in a position to get to the shot – no let.

Note: This can occur if a player plays a winning drop-shot into the dead nick and then fails to clear the shot. Because there is no chance of the opponent getting the ball back there would be no let. It also occurs when a player jumps over the ball. If the opponent is nowhere near and has no chance of getting the ball, its being jumped over is irrelevant. However, if the opponent is in a position to strike, he should be awarded the stroke.

Time wasting

Players must not waste time, either by prolonging discussion with the referee or by being slow returning to court after the interval between games. If a player persists in time wasting, after a warning, a game may be awarded to the opponent.

Disqualification

The referee has the power to disqualify a player if he continues to infringe the rules, after due warning.

Injury

A player may leave the court in the event of an injury caused by the opponent. If the match is recommenced the same day, the players will resume where play left off. If the match is resumed on another day, the game is restarted unless both players agree otherwise.

Methods of recording the score

Player A	$0^R 1^L$		$1^L 2^R 3^L 4^R 5^{Lf} 6^R 7^L 8^R 9$
Player B		$0_R 1_L 2_{Rf} 3_L$	

A starts out by serving from the right. He takes the first point and then serves from the left. He loses this point and B serves from the right. B wins three points, in spite of serving a single service fault with the score at 2 – 1. B then serves his hand out and, with the score at 1 – 3, A serves again from the left. A goes on to take the next eight points and win the game, 9-3.

Player A	Player B
0–0R	
1–0L	
2–0R	
	0–2R
	1–2Lf
2–1R	
3–1L	
4–1R	
5–1L	
6–1R	
7–1L	
8–1R	
9–1 Game	

A wins the first two points and then serves his hand out while serving from the right. B wins a point, serving from the right, but then serves a fault and goes on to lose the next point. The service reverts to A, who wins the game, 9 – 1.

The doubles game

As mentioned previously it is possible to play squash as a doubles game, with two players in each team. There are a small number of special doubles courts, which are larger in dimension than the normal singles court but doubles can be played in the conventional, singles squash court. The doubles game is fun if played well and safely. Avoid players with large swings.

The following rules of the game will be of help if you plan to experiment in the art of doubles.

Scoring

Every point is scored whether you are 'hand in' or 'hand out'. A normal doubles match is the best of five games and the game is played to fifteen points, except that:

a) at 13 all the side which first reached the score of 13 must elect one of the following before the next serve –
(i) set to five points, making the game 18 points,
(ii) set to three points, making the game 16 points,
(iii) no set, in which case the game remains at 15 points;
b) At 14 all, provided the score has not been 13 all, the side which first reached the score of 14 must elect one of the following before the next serve –
(i) set to three points, making the game 17 points,
(ii) no set, in which case the game remains at 15 points.

Service

As in badminton, the serving side has two 'hands', apart from at the beginning of each game, when the service changes immediately the server loses the first point. The order of serving within the partnership must not be altered during a game. The two partners of a side shall serve in succession, the first retaining his serve until he loses a point. When his partner loses the next point, the serve reverts to the opponents. The rules on service are similar to those for the singles game, except that when the ball is struck on or above the boundary line it is only counted as a single fault.

Return of service

At the beginning of each game each side shall designate one of its players to receive service from the right-hand box and the other to receive from the left-hand box. It is not possible to alter this arrangement during a game. If a service is called a fault it is not possible for the receiver to take the service.

Let

A let should be played whenever a player is prevented from either playing or seeing the ball, due to the position of one of the opponents.

Note: There are certain rules concerning deliberate baulking which may allow a point to be awarded, but in the early stages of doubles it is far better to stop and play a let.

Being hit by the ball

If you are hit by the ball as it travels towards the front wall, either on a direct hit or from the other walls, a let shall be played, providing the ball would have reached the front wall. If you hit your partner with the ball, it is a point to the other side, unless your partner was unable to get out of the line of the ball because of an opponent's position. If a player is hit by the ball as it travels from the front wall, it is a point to the opponents, unless he was prevented from getting out of the line of the ball by one of the opponents.

The American game

The game of squash played in the USA and parts of Canada and South America is slightly different to the 'soft ball' game known as the British game, which is played in nearly all other parts of the world, including the great squash playing countries of Australia, New Zealand, Pakistan, India, South Africa and, last but not least, Great Britain itself.

The court

The American court is somewhat narrower than the more usual, British court.

Floor and wall markings

Both the tin and the cut line are slightly higher and the side boundary line is positioned differently (Fig. 70). The service boxes are far smaller since, because the court is narrower, the server has to start much closer to the sidewall in order to give his opponent room to play the return.

The ball

The ball is made of hard, solid rubber and is very bouncy. It is slightly larger than the 'soft' squash ball and very similar to a lacrosse ball.

The racket

The racket is similar to the one used for the British game, but, in order to cope with the harder ball, it is heavier and in every aspect more sturdy.

The score

Every point is scored whether the player is 'hand in' or 'hand out'. A normal match is the best of five games and the game is played to fifteen points, except that:
a) at 13 all the receiver chooses one of the following –
(i) set to five points, making the game 18 points,
(ii) set to three points, making the game 16 points,
(iii) no set, in which case the game remains at 15 points;
b) at 14 all, provided the score has not been 13 all, the receiver elects one of the following –
(i) set to three points, making the game 17 points,
(ii) no set, in which case the game remains at 15 points.

The aim of the game

Fundamentally the American and British games are the same and tactics similar. A controlled, tight length shot is extremely effective if played well, but, because of the nature of the ball, a poorly placed shot in the middle of the court will usually be 'murdered' by the opponent. The boast from the back corners is not used to a great extent, as most balls played to the back of the court rebound off the back wall almost as far forward as the short line, making it possible for a drive to be played directly to the front wall. The use of the lob service, and the lob itself, is most effective in order to slow down the game. The American game is generally less demanding physically than the British, with less movement up and down the court and a smaller area to cover.

The rules book

Copies of the rules of both the singles and doubles game and the American game may be obtained from the Squash Rackets Association and the Women's Squash Rackets Association (addresses on p. 94).

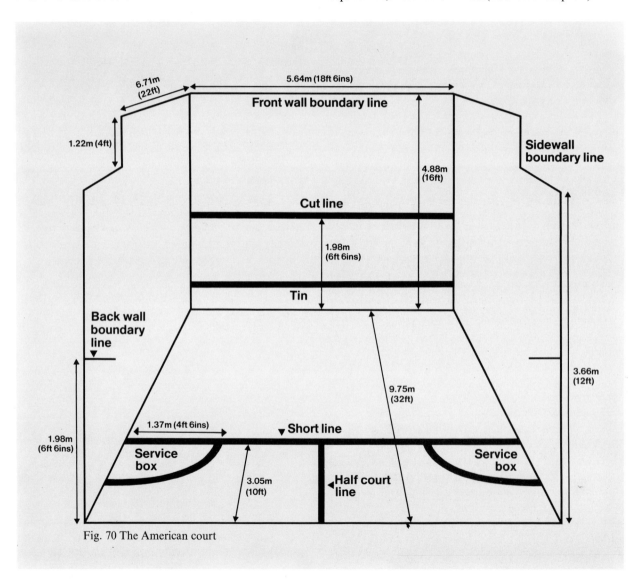

Fig. 70 The American court

Chapter 8 Equipment

While it is true to say that good equipment alone will not necessarily improve your game, careful selection of what is required will help, whether through the good feel of the racket or the comfort and style of your squash 'gear'.

Choosing a racket

There are a large number of rackets on the market and all manufacturers will claim to have the perfect model for every customer, so remember when choosing your new racket that it should mould comfortably into your hand and, rather like a pair of shoes, should feel a part of you. Always swing the racket using your squash swing to help you decide whether the balance and weight are right for you. Avoid rackets which are too heavy and clublike.

Type of shaft

You will soon discover that not all rackets are made of wood throughout. A number will have a steel shaft and others may have a glass fibre shaft. Select the one that appeals to you, but bear in mind that virtually every top player uses a shaft made entirely of wood – you could do worse than follow their example. Wood tends to give better feel and touch. The head of the racket *must* be made of wood. Steel headed rackets are not allowed according to the rules of the game.

Stringing

Most top quality rackets are strung with natural gut. This does tend to break but will feel good to play with. Gut can be strung more tightly than synthetics, but, since it is a natural fibre, it will begin to lose its tension after a period of play.

Synthetic strings are used in the majority of rackets now on the market. These are more reliable than gut but will not give you quite the same feel of the ball on the racket. However, at all levels of play, synthetic stringing is quite acceptable.

Length of grip

It is possible to purchase a racket with either a short or long grip. This is largely a matter of individual preference depending on the size of the player's hands.

Type of grip

Racket grips are made from leather, reversed calf, towel, adhesive linen, aquagrips and so on – quite a choice. The type of grip selected is again a matter of individual preference. If you play in a club with warm courts and find that your hand becomes hot and sticky it is probably wise to use a grip which will give you a firm hold on the racket; towelling, adhesive linen or aquagrip might be the best. These types of grip do need renewing fairly regularly however.

Weight of racket

Manufacturers offer a wide choice of shaft, stringing and type of grip, but the actual weight and grip size of the racket tend to be thought out for you and it is

unusual to find a selection of either grip sizes or weights. However, models do vary so once again it is a question of selecting the right racket for you. Don't let anyone else choose your racket. You are the one who will have to play with it.

Clothing

The rules state clearly that white clothing must be worn on the squash court and a coloured trim of only a 5cm (2ins) border or less is permissible on clothing, socks or shoes. There is a wide range of clothing from which to choose, but perhaps the three most important points to remember when selecting your outfit are (i) comfort, (ii) ability to absorb perspiration and (iii) the right 'look' for you. A tracksuit is a good investment as it can be worn in the knock-up as well as during that all-important off-court training.

Shoes

It is essential that your shoes should fit well and provide you with a good grip. As with all other sport-

ing equipment, there is a vast range of sporting footwear from which to choose. Select shoes that are comfortable, but bear in mind that speed about the court is all-important, so don't wear a pair which will slow your footwork down.

Socks

As good movement is so essential when playing squash, it is important to select a pair of socks which will be fully absorbent. Nylon is not recommended, as it can cause blisters – the dreaded affliction of many a squash player. So, wear predominantly woollen socks and if you do suffer from blisters take a tip from the top players and wear two pairs when playing.

Headbands, sweatlets, etc.

All these additional aids to successful squash are available for those who feel they need them. It is far better to wear a towel headband than spend the entire match flicking your hair out of your eyes. Good visibility is just as important as good mobility.

Chapter 9 **Competitive play**

The first step towards serious competitive play is to join a club, either a private members' club, a commercial club, or perhaps a club formed within a sports centre. Details of all clubs can be obtained through the national governing bodies – the Squash Rackets Association (SRA), or the Women's Squash Rackets Association (WSRA). Nearly all clubs are affiliated to one or other of these bodies.

Most clubs will have a full membership, but you can have your name put on the waiting list and you will not usually have to wait for more than one season. Clubs often offer some form of restricted membership if their normal membership is full and this is well worth considering, especially if you are able to play during the day or at weekends.

Subscriptions to squash clubs vary considerably. Clubs which are run and owned by the members themselves are often less expensive than the new clubs opened by commercial proprietors, who are obviously anxious to get a good return on their initial investment. Many members' clubs have additional sporting facilities, such as tennis courts and rugby pitches. Squash is a game which fits in well with these other activities and keeps a club 'ticking over' in the off season. You will often have to pay a court booking fee and a charge for the use of the lights in addition to the annual squash subscription. Such charges again vary widely, from well below a pound to well over per forty minute booking. In view of this difference in costs, it is obviously important to select a club which will really suit you. Many of the more sophisticated clubs in big cities have excellent bar and restaurant facilities, whereas the smaller clubs usually have fewer 'services' to offer.

From the competitive aspect of the game, most clubs, and this includes clubs in many sports centres, run some form of competitive league or ladder, and it is well worth putting your name down for this. A ladder gives you the opportunity to work your way up gradually, playing opponents who are slightly higher on the list. Most ladders allow one free challenge match for you to get yourself on the ladder and you then challenge any one of the three players placed above you. If you beat any one of them you go above them. Anyone placed below you may challenge you in the same way.

A league is usually arranged according to standard and will have five or six players in each division who must play each other over a period of five to six weeks. On completion, the two players with the most wins will be promoted to the division above and the two players with the least number of wins will be relegated. This gives you the opportunity of playing another group of opponents in the next league period. Internal league matches are a good training ground for club matches against outside opposition, as you will soon discover that there is far more intense competition in a league match than in a 'friendly'.

Most clubs use their internal league results as a guide to selection for teams for inter-club league matches. These are normally run by the county associations, and vary somewhat in format around the country. Many clubs will have two or three teams playing in different divisions in the league, so this spreads the competitive experience at varying levels throughout a club – competitive squash is not just for the very good. Most teams consist of four or five players depending on the rules of the competition and, with six or seven teams in a division, matches are normally played on a home and away basis giving each club team approximately fourteen matches in one season. In Great Britain the squash season runs from about September until April, although many clubs now run summer leagues as well.

Apart from the inter-club league run on a county basis, there are a number of inter-club knock-out events which are run on a national basis. These are normally sponsored events and are run for both men's and women's teams. Some are open to mixed teams. In the early rounds matches are played within an area, and it is only if your team wins through to the later rounds that you have to travel further afield.

The competitive structure

World championships
Team event – Individual event

International selection
National competitions

External county competitions
Inter-county leagues – Open tournaments
National club competitions

Internal county competitions
Inter-club leagues – County closed championships

Club
Ladder – League – Tournament

In addition to external club competition, most clubs run some form of internal club championships during the winter season. These often follow much the same pattern as a major tournament, being played over a weekend on a knock-out basis. Plate events are usually run for players who lose early on in the competition, so you are guaranteed a minimum of two matches.

The next stage in the development of the competitive player would be through county competition. Most counties run a knock-out tournament for players who are qualified to play for that county, either by residence of more than a year or by having been born there. In addition to this county closed tournament, many of the larger counties run a county ladder, similar to a club ladder. This gives up-and-coming players the chance to challenge those already established in the county game.

The Squash Rackets Association and the Women's Squash Rackets Association run an inter-county league competition, consisting of teams from all counties. The men's competition is simply for the first county teams, but for the women's event counties are allowed to enter two or three teams which are then put into divisions according to merit. Again these leagues are run on a promotion and relegation basis at the end of the season and they give county competition to a wide variety of players, as the standard throughout the country varies considerably.

Knock-out tournaments are staged throughout the country, usually over a weekend, and many of these will accept entries from local players. Large tournaments are often divided into A and B sections, so again you are grouped roughly according to your ability. This is important, as there is nothing more unrewarding than being removed from the squash court in a matter of minutes by an opponent who is quite out of your class. Far better to work your way gradually up this 'ladder to success'.

In the top men's game there is at present a distinction between the amateur player and the professional and although some competitions are open to both, many are still restricted events. The women's game in Great Britain has now become 'open', i.e. events are open to all players.

Who controls the game?
The game of squash rackets is administered by the International Squash Federation, which consists of members elected from all squash playing countries. In Great Britain there are two national governing bodies of the sport, the Squash Rackets Association (SRA), which represents the men's game, and the Women's Squash Rackets Association (WSRA), which is responsible for the development of the women's game. The associations liaise on many aspects of the game and are responsible for the development of the game at all levels, from the staging and organising of the top national championships, whether open or closed, to the training of coaches, referees and markers, and coaching of top players at both senior and junior level. Both associations have a national coach.

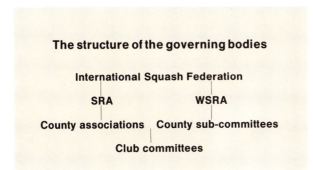

The structure of the governing bodies

International Squash Federation

SRA   WSRA

County associations   County sub-committees

Club committees

The junior game

Far more squash is now being played at a younger age, both in schools and in clubs. Consequently, more competitive squash has emerged at the younger age level.

Both national associations run a Junior Proficiency Certificate and many young players now sport a squash badge on their tracksuit. The Junior Proficiency Certificate is divided into three sections – Elementary, Intermediate and Advanced – and examines players on their ability to play the basic shots

The junior competitive and selected coaching structure

International
Tours – Competitions – Squads

National
Inter-county – Open – Selected national
competition tournaments and area training

County
Junior – Inter-club – Selected
championships league county training

Club   School
Ladder – League – Tournament – 'Friendly' matches
Inter-schools knock-out tournaments
Proficiency certificates

of the game effectively. The examination for these certificates may be taken by qualified SRA or WSRA coaches.

Competition for junior players includes a national inter-schools knock-out competition for boys and girls, a junior inter-county league run on similar lines to the senior league and, in some parts of the country, a junior inter-club league. Tournaments at both county and national level are also held and run on a knock-out basis.

Many talented junior players, both boys and girls, are selected under the SRA and WSRA training schemes to have additional coaching through membership of national junior squads. From these squads, the national junior teams are selected for matches against other countries, played both at home and on tour in places such as Australia, South Africa, the USA and Europe.

The coaching structure

You will often see notices on club or sports centre notice boards advertising coaching by a 'qualified coach'. It is useful to know the various levels of coaching certificates necessary in order for a person to be able to coach squash effectively.

Both the SRA and WSRA run a coaching scheme which qualifies coaches at two levels – the elementary level and the advanced or senior level. The professional qualification, the third and final stage of this structure, is administered by the Squash Rackets Professionals' Association (SRPA). Coaches should qualify at all three levels before calling themselves qualified professional coaches.

The Elementary Certificate is designed to give coaches a sound knowledge of the techniques of the game for coaching beginners and organising a group coaching session. The Advanced or Senior Certificate concentrates on the more advanced techniques and the coaching of the better pupil on a more individual basis. Both certificates require a competent playing standard from the coach, with particular emphasis

---

The coaching structure

Professional coach (SRPA)

Advanced coach (SRA)   Advanced coach (WSRA)

Intermediate coach (WSRA)

Elementary coach (SRA)   Elementary coach (WSRA)

SRPA   Squash Rackets Professionals' Association
SRA   Squash Rackets Association
WSRA   Women's Squash Rackets Association

---

on good demonstrations of the shot to be taught and the ability to 'feed' the pupil correctly. Coaches must also have a sound knowledge of the rules of the game and prove themselves to be competent at marking and refereeing.

At the professional level a very high degree of competence is required in all aspects of teaching and playing the game.

Watching the top game

Squash is now reputed to be the largest participant sport in Great Britain and, although it falls far behind others as a spectator sport, it is certainly worth watching the top players in action if you get the opportunity.

Many of the top world events are staged in Britain and it is often possible to get tickets to watch them 'live'. The World Championships are held once every two to three years, though not always in this country. Details of major competitions can be obtained from the SRA and WSRA.

Many of the national events, such as the British Open Championships, the British Amateur Championships and the Women's Open Championships are staged at the National Squash Centre at Wembley Stadium. Other events, such as the British Men's Closed and the British Women's Closed tend to be held at venues outside London, thus taking top competitive squash to areas all over the country.

Overseas the game is growing tremendously, particularly in Europe and North America. More and more interest is being shown in the English game in the USA and a lighter racket and the softer ball are being used. As in many professional sports, an international circuit has been formed for the top world-class players, and you can see these players in action during events staged in this country. Jonah Barrington, former British Amateur Champion from 1966 to 1968 and British Open Champion from 1966 to 1967 and 1969 to 1972, has perhaps done more for the growth of the game in this country than anyone else, and he is Chairman of the International Squash Players Association. A Women's International Squash Players Association has also been formed and is currently organising an international circuit for the top women players throughout the world.

Since squash is a fairly young game compared with many other sports, it does not always get a realistic share of coverage in the media. At present very little squash is shown on national television, though as more and more courts are built with viewing facilities the situation should improve. It *is* possible to follow the results of major events if you read the small print carefully, and there are now a number of good monthly publications on squash which will give you reports on tournament play, coaching techniques, training methods, news and views, etc. It is not wise to be too subjective about your squash and an attempt to broaden your knowledge, whether on a specific technical point or in general, will never be wasted.

Addresses

The Squash Rackets Association
70 Brompton Road, London SW3 1DX

The Women's Squash Rackets Association
345 Upper Richmond Road West
Sheen, London SW14 8QN

The Squash Rackets Professionals' Association
127 Old Bath Road, Cheltenham, Glos.

Index